CONESTOGA WAGON
1750-1850

FREIGHT CARRIER FOR 100 YEARS OF AMERICA'S WESTWARD EXPANSION

By George Shumway, Edward Durell, Howard C. Frey

Early America needed an all-purpose vehicle to haul furs, trade goods, farm produce, and freight, so she developed the famous Conestoga wagon. During the century of expansion from 1750 to 1850, when the frontier moved from the Appalachian piedmont to the far west, this wagon was the chief means of overland freight transport.

The Conestoga wagon originated in the Pennsylvania Dutch section of southeastern Pennsylvania between 1720 and 1750. Its first uses were to haul farm produce from outlying counties to Philadelphia and to back load with manufactured goods from the city or from Europe. In great numbers they went with General Braddock, over incredibly rough roads, to his defeat in the wilderness, and then with Forbes on his successful push to Pittsburgh a few years later. During the Revolutionary War Pennsylvania supplied most of the wagons used by the American army, and these were Conestogas.

After the Revolution settlers streamed into the Ohio Valley via the few poor roads that crossed the mountains. The Conestoga became the important transportation link between the east and the new west, and it carried an ever-increasing freight traffic as western settlement continued and as roads improved. In the decades after 1815 trans-mountain freighting came into its greatest glory as Conestogas by the thousands jammed the roads to Pittsburgh and Wheeling. The picturesque days of the Conestoga ended abruptly in mid-century when railroad lines to the Ohio Valley were completed.

The Conestoga wagon is a distinctly American vehicle, developed to meet the rugged requirements of the frontier. Its structure is complex and its form is graceful.

CONESTOGA WAGON 1750-1850

Freight Carrier for 100 Years of
America's Westward Expansion

by

George Shumway, Edward Durell, Howard C. Frey

Published jointly by

EARLY AMERICAN INDUSTRIES ASSOCIATION, INC.
and GEORGE SHUMWAY

© George Shumway 1964

Library of Congress Catalog Card Number 64-22827

Printed in the United States of America

1500 Copies Printed at York, Pennsylvania

by TRIMMER PRINTING, INC., 1964

Address correspondence to

George Shumway, *Publisher*

R. D. 7, York, Pennsylvania

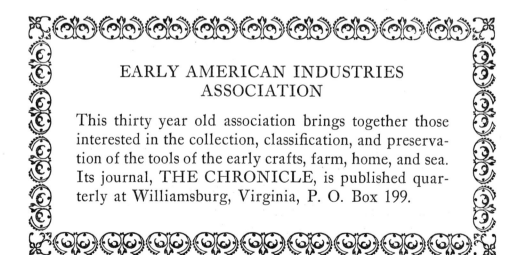

EARLY AMERICAN INDUSTRIES
ASSOCIATION

This thirty year old association brings together those interested in the collection, classification, and preservation of the tools of the early crafts, farm, home, and sea. Its journal, THE CHRONICLE, is published quarterly at Williamsburg, Virginia, P. O. Box 199.

Pennsylvania's Conestoga Wagons *did most of the freight hauling for the American forces during the Revolutionary War. Nick Eggenhofer made the dramatic drawing used for the end plates, which shows a wagon as it might have appeared at that time. He emphasized the great power of the team of six large Conestoga horses.*

FOREWORD

On August 31st, 1933, at Northampton, Massachusetts, sixteen avid collectors of early American "tools, implements, utensils, instruments, vehicles and mechanical devices" formed the Early American Industries Association, with the declared purpose of encouraging "the study and better understanding of early American industry." Within three months, the first issue of *The Chronicle* appeared — dramatic evidence of their determination to record and disseminate little known facts pertaining to early trades and crafts. Thirty years later, *The Chronicle* still is published regularly, and considered by many to be the authority in its field.

"The Early American Industries Association, Inc., is a non-profit organization of more than twenty-five years standing. Memberships include collectors, museums, dealers, libraries and historical societies.

The purpose of the Association is to encourage a better understanding and appreciation of early American industry in the home, on the farm, in the shop, and on the sea. Through its members it seeks to discover, identify, classify, preserve and exhibit the old tools, implements, utensils, instruments, vehicles and mechanical devices made and used by our forefathers."

For many years, EAIA members have realized that a more comprehensive publications program was desirable to more completely study and record the history of tools and industries in America. In the fall of 1958, at our twenty-fifth anniversary meeting, the Publications Committee was formed, and the Association embarked on this, its first book publishing effort. Under the dedicated leadership of its chairman, Mr. Edward Durell, the subject of the Conestoga wagon was selected, and the accumulation of data for a manuscript began.

While it is true (for obvious reasons) that only a few EAIA members have Conestoga wagons in their collections, many do prize beautiful examples of the wagon's wrought iron hardware, its dated and sometimes signed jacks, and its tar pots. And because early transportation generally is recognized as the backbone of commerce prior to the industrial revolution, the history of the Conestoga wagon seemed a fitting subject for our first book.

v

The Association was fortunate in being able to purchase a preliminary manuscript from Mr. Howard C. Frey who had participated in the collection of data for a book about the Conestoga wagon published in 1930 by John Omwake, and long since out of print. Further work on the project was done over a period of many months by Mr. Gordon Manning. In 1963 Dr. George Shumway agreed to complete the desired research, prepare the final manuscript, and then join the Association in publishing the book.

In spite of the important contributions of these men, the Conestoga wagon book would not yet be "rolling" were it not for the many EAIA members who have helped so much during the five-year undertaking. Proper recognition would sound almost like the membership roster, but special thanks go to the long-suffering Publications Committee, made up of Miner J. Cooper, William D. Geiger, Ralph Hodgkinson, the late Laurence Johnson, James A. Keillor, Loring McMillen, Mrs. Josephine Pierce, Dr. Fred C. Sabin, John Still, Raymond R. Townsend, Minor Wine Thomas, Jr., and Frank Wildung. Most of all, however, the Association is indebted to Edward Durell, for it was through his determination, persistence and enthusiasm that it is possible for CONESTOGA WAGON 1750-1850 to arrive "with bells on".

Lawrence S. Cooke, President
Early American Industries Association, Inc.

PREFACE

We who have grown up in the United States of the mid-twentieth century, with our electrical conveniences, cars, television sets, and innumerable other factory products, our ever-present public utilities, public health services, and welfare agencies, look back in history with a certain awe at those long ago times when our forefathers settled this land by means of hard work, using their bare hands and a few simple tools. We think of the unsettled times of the eighteenth century when British, French, Indian, and American forces struggled with one another for control of the lands, and we feel secure in our well-ordered, peaceful land. But in some respects we of the twentieth century live in a much more unsettling time, for we now are in the midst of an earthwide revolution in which a rapidly growing technological complex separates us farther and farther from the relatively simple life of times past, and in which a population explosion threatens not only to deprive us of decent living space, but even to deprive us of standing room on the continents.

This revolution has prospered at the expense of the integrity in our lives. Nearly every article which we now use is the product of the machine age, and as a result we have lost an ability to care much for certain aspects of quality that only careful handwork could impart to manufactured articles. So often we are willing to settle for whatever will do the minimum job, or for whatever will do the job at the absolute minimum cost. If the outside looks all right, and the inside works, little else matters. And so often we are willing to regard the means to the end as unimportant. The craftsman, or artisan, of old derived pleasure and life from his work; his counterpart of today, the factory worker, has no great enthusiasm for his work, and derives little from it other than his security in the form of a regular pay check.

The world of the past is one place where an individual can go to search for, and probably find, some of this lost integrity. And one way this may be done is through detailed study of the well-made products of the handicraft age, together with the methods of manufacture, the uses to which they were put, and their place in history.

The Conestoga wagon is a most worthy subject for study, for in addition to being a work of art in wood and iron, it has a long history of useful service to a young and growing country. It began as a farm wagon for the German and English settlers of southeastern Pennsylvania in the early eighteenth century. It proved so reliable that it still was in use and still being manufactured in essentially unchanged form a century later. After suitable roads were opened up, it became the chief means of transporting freight from the eastern seaboard across the mountains to the rapidly developing communities of the Ohio Valley. This remarkable wagon was built through the cooperative efforts of blacksmiths and wagon makers, who did more than merely manufacture it. They created it, from the iron of Pennsylvania's forges and the wood of her forests. They were not content merely to make a serviceable vehicle; it had to look like something too. So they took care with the architectural design of it, and they embellished it by carving the wood and by artfully shaping the necessary and functional ironwork.

The Conestoga wagon has not been a forgotten subject to those interested in our country's early history. A number of wagons now are preserved in historical societies, and in museums both public and private, and still others are in the hands of private owners who cherish them. The decorative ironwork from wagons that have been broken up is valued by collectors and often brings a relatively high price on the antique market. Numerous articles about the wagon have been written for newspapers and magazines, but as is usually the case with publication in periodicals, these now are essentially lost to all except the diligent researcher willing to dig them out. The one and only book which has been produced to tell the story of the wagon was published in 1930 by John Omwake for private distribution. This is entitled *The Conestoga Six-Horse Bell Teams of Eastern Pennsylvania,* and it was produced through the collaboration of Mr. H. K. Landis, one of the founders of the Pennsylvania Farm Museum of Landis Valley, Miss Catherine P. Hargrave, and Mr. Howard C. Frey. This book was printed in small quantity and long has been difficult to acquire.

The story of the Conestoga wagon needs to be told, and it needs to be available in book form. A number of years ago the Early American Industries Association undertook the task of putting together a book about the wagon which would supersede the earlier book published by Omwake. Mr. Edward Durell was the moving force behind this project, and through his persistent efforts a manuscript began to take form. Fortunately, Mr. Howard C. Frey, who helped produce the earlier book, and who is now a man of seventy two years, has been able to contribute to this present undertaking. Mr. Frey has spent his life in the land of the Conestoga wagon and always has been an admirer and student of the old wagon and its history. He knew people who used the wagons for their farm work and for their freight hauling, and from these people he learned details about wagoning that never got recorded in times past because they were so commonplace that no one bothered to write them down, and which would be all but impossible for someone to find today by searching through old records.

I entered the picture after a rough manuscript had been put together and many of the illustrations had been collected. As I worked with the available data, many unanswered questions came to my mind, so I attempted to answer some of these through my own research efforts. Eventually I began to long for a fine Conestoga wagon to keep in the old barn on my York County farm, and to collect wagon parts. One day Howard Frey took me out to an old barn near Dover and pointed up toward the rafters. There were the two sides of a once-beautiful Conestoga, being used as part of a platform for hay. These were purchased and carried home, with the intention of restoring a wagon from them. Only by working on such a restoration, or by building a wagon from scratch, does one really get an adequate understanding of their construction. I gained an appreciation for the wagon that I would not have had otherwise through this work.

I have worked on all chapters of this book except numbers 10 and 13 which bear their author's names. Chapters 1, 2, 3, 4, 8, 14, 15, and 16 are my own new contributions.

The kind of story that this book has to tell rarely ever is completed, and so it is that additional bits of information about the Conestoga wagon will turn up from time to time. To be practical, the research must be terminated eventually, and the manuscript sent to press. Nevertheless, with the future in mind, I will continue to collect information about the grand old wagon, and would appreciate having such information called to my attention by others. Information from the eighteenth century is particularly important and in short supply.

George Shumway
York, Pennsylvania

31 March, 1964

CONTENTS

Chapter 1
The Conestoga Wagon—A Definition

A FTER the American Revolutionary War drew to a close, settlers flocked into the Ohio River Valley. Many went to claim land given to them in partial payment for war services, and still others went to buy land cheaper than it could be had in the well-settled regions east of the mountains. The Ohio Valley bloomed with settlement, and by the end of the century the Valley had become almost a separate country, isolated from the east by the mountain barrier.

Settlers poured over the mountains, taking with them what they could in the way of possessions, and taking with them also a need for a thousand and one other things they could not carry. Pittsburgh and Wheeling were the ports of entry. Between these cities of the west and the old established seaboard cities of the east, particularly Philadelphia and Baltimore, a heavy trade developed. This trade was possible only because of the inland ship of commerce, or Conestoga wagon, that lumbered back and forth across the mountains, for there were no rivers or canals going in the right direction, and until about 1850 there were no railroads.

In addition to this traffic with the Ohio Valley, Philadelphia and Baltimore carried on a profitable commerce with the prosperous region that lay between them and the mountains, containing long-established towns such as Allentown, Reading, Lancaster, York, Harrisburg, Chambersburg, and Hagerstown. The farmers there were able to produce such surpluses that they needed good wagons to carry their crops to market, and the wagons they used were Conestoga wagons.

Conestoga wagoning had its peak of activity in the years between 1820 and 1840. The main wagon routes in that period were crowded with the large wagons carrying their characteristic white cloth tops, and pulled by teams of four, five, or six horses. So heavy was the traffic that wagoners sometimes had to wait in line for three days before their turns came to be ferried across the Susquehanna River.

With the coming of the railroads in the mid-nineteenth century, long-distance hauling by Conestoga wagon came to an abrupt end, and by the time of the Civil War, Conestoga wagoning was regarded as a romantic episode of recent history. Wagons continued to be used for short-distance freight hauling to places not touched by the railroads, and farmers continued to use wagons to haul their crops and for other farm work. And in the far west settlers continued to push on to new lands in their covered wagons. But these freight wagons and farm wagons of the post-Civil War period, and the covered wagons of the west, were not Conestogas. Of course old Conestogas continued to be used as long as they were serviceable, and some of these traveled far from their homeland.

The classical Conestoga wagon was not simply a wagon. It was a beautiful wagon. This beauty was planned for in the designing of the vehicle and carried out in the making of it. Manufacture of the Conestoga wagon was centered in southeastern Pennsylvania, a region blessed with a favorable climate, agricultural prosperity, and a population capable both of appreciating beauty and of creating it through their handwork. It was here that the lovely Pennsylvania longrifle originated and was brought to its artistic high-point. Here also were built the handsome stone houses and fine barns that have stood the test of time so well. And here, too, the famous Pennsylvania Dutch folk art came into being, for this was the land of the Pennsylvania Dutch.

After Conestoga wagoning drew to a close in the middle of the century, the need for farm and freight wagons continued. Wagon makers who once had built Conestogas began producing simpler wagons more suited to the needs of the times. These makers had more than a century of tradition and experience behind them, so the new wagons they produced retained many features of the Conestogas, but lacked other features that no longer were useful, such as the bows and bow staples, the toolbox, the feedbox and feedbox chains, or the axe and axe holder. These later wagons are not Conestogas, although in recent years the name has been applied wishfully to some of them. A line must be drawn somewhere.

With the coming of the automobile, the wagons that so long had been preserved in the barns of Pennsylvania became useless occupiers of space, so by the hundreds they were hauled out and left in the fields to rot. The number of good Conestogas that have survived until the

FIGURE 1. A Conestoga wagon of Pennsylvania and a six-horse team, with bells. This photograph was taken in 1906 when the wagon was owned by the Orndorff family of Franklin County. *Penna. Farm Museum of Landis Valley.*

FIGURE 2. One of the largest of the Conestoga freighters, this is known as the Burgner wagon. The cloth cover is supported by thirteen bows. *Penna. Farm Museum of Landis Valley.*

FIGURE 3. A Conestoga wagon and six horse team photographed in 1908 when they were used in a pageant by the Pennsylvania Railroad. *The National Geographic Society, Washington, D. C.*

PHILADELPHIA PITTSBURG 20 DAYS

5

FIGURE 4. An unidentified Conestoga wagon on the streets of Lancaster, Pa., in 1908. Many Conestoga wagon boxes have a more pronounced curvature to their sides than does this one. *Penna. Farm Museum of Landis Valley.*

FIGURE 5. This beautifully proportioned Conestoga is known as the Amos Gingrich wagon. It is shown here in front of the Oreville Hotel in about 1913. The horses belonged to a contractor named Shaub. *Penna. Farm Museum of Landis Valley.*

FIGURE 6. In 1813 a number of Conestoga wagons were used to carry cannon powder from the Du Pont factory in Wilmington, Delaware, to Commodore Perry's fleet on the Great Lakes. In 1913 (when this photograph was taken) this, the Gingrich wagon, was driven to Erie as part of the centennial celebration. This handsome wagon is a classic example of the Conestoga at its best. Presently it is on display at the Pennsylvania Farm Museum of Landis Valley. *Reproduced from the Collections of the Library of Congress.*

FIGURE 7. The Gingrich wagon is one of the finest remaining examples of a Conestoga wagon. The superior design and proportioning of this wagon, and of a number of others, is proof enough that beauty as well as utility was desired in a Conestoga wagon. Note that the 1913 photograph (FIG. 6) shows what apparently are the original bows, with flattened tops, to support the cloth cover, whereas the last two bows shown here are replacements which lack the flattened tops, and as a consequence, some of the original beauty has been lost. *Photo by Karl G. Rath, Harrisburg, Pa., courtesy Penna. Farm Museum of Landis Valley.*

9

Figure 8. The Thuma wagon and a team of six mules is shown in this photograph, taken in front of the Capitol at Harrisburg about 1929.

present day is small compared with the vast numbers of them that once existed. The remaining Conestogas probably number less than one hundred fifty. Of these, about thirty-five are preserved in museums, another thirty-five are in the possession of appreciative owners, and fifty or more probably exist hidden away in the barns of Pennsylvania and nearby states, yet to be discovered. Thus it behooves us to cherish the few that remain, and to repair and restore those that need it.

Some of the outstanding features of a Conestoga wagon, such as the cloth cover supported by wooden bows, and the curved bed with up-swept bow and stern, are readily apparent even to the untrained eye. But to appreciate better one of these wagons, a number of other features must be noted also. In spite of the fact that Conestogas were made in a great many individual shops, and over a long range of time, there were many features that they possessed in common. These features distinguish a Conestoga from its cousins of the late nineteenth century. The minor details of Conestogas vary from wagon to wagon, but the wagons are remarkably consistent in possessing the group of features given in the following list.

It should be noted that the bed or box of a wagon is a separate unit which merely rests upon the wheel-and-axle assemblies, called running gear. Boxes and running gear are more or less interchangeable. The attrition rate for running gear has been higher than that for boxes, hence existing Conestoga boxes may not be with the original running gears for which they were made.

CHARACTERISTIC FEATURES OF A
CONESTOGA WAGON
BOX or BED

Cloth cover to protect wagon contents.

Bows of bent wood to support the cloth cover, numbering between 8 and 12.

Staples of iron in the top and middle side rails to hold the bows.

Side panels with curved profile, swept up at front and rear, top and bottom rails.

Sides constructed of three more or less horizontal rails and 8 to 12 more or less upright standards, with the space between the rails filled with boards.

Front end panel not vertical, but slanting, and fastened with pins to extensions of top side rails. Top half sometimes removable.

Decorative chip carving on extreme edges of front end panel and
rear end gate.

Top rail and middle rail of front end panel downbowed in the middle.

Rear end gate not vertical, but slanting, removable, and fastened at
the top with pins to extensions of the top side rails.

Top rail and middle rail of rear end gate bowed upward for the sake
of appearance.

Tool box on left side.

Front bolster permanently fastened to box.

Feedbox support chains fastened to top rail at rear.

Lazy-board.

RUNNING GEAR

Rear wheels 54 inches in diameter, or greater, and containing 14 or
16 spokes.

Linch pins for holding wheels to axles.

Axles of wood, shod top and bottom with iron clouts, but not completely sheathed with a skein.

Tongue, one horse in length, rigidly fixed to front hounds.

Axe sheath of iron, and axe handle ring, on left front hound.

Rear hounds fastened to rear axletree by iron hound pins.

Brake mechanism, if present, operated by long iron lever on left side,
and no original provision made for later type of rear brake lever.

Tar pot hook and staple.

Iron hub caps over the ends of wheel hubs.

Staple in tongue for feedbox lug.

Certainly not every Conestoga wagon possessed all of the features
mentioned, but most of them did. Occasionally a Conestoga was built
without a toolbox, or without a lazy-board. But a wagon which has
a flat floor, straight bottom side rails, and which lacks feedbox chains
and staples for bows, probably does not deserve the name of Conestoga. And of course not all wagons made in the century before 1850
were Conestogas. Many undoubtedly were of simpler construction
and intended for farm or emigrant use.

Although southeastern Pennsylvania was the center for the manufacture of Conestoga wagons, they undoubtedly were made and used
also in the neighboring states of New Jersey, Maryland, Virginia,

Ohio, and probably also in the Carolinas where people from Pennsylvania settled at an early date. Emigrants from Pennsylvania took Conestogas to Ontario in the 1790's, and used them there for farm vehicles.[1]

REFERENCE—

1. Reaman, G. Elmore (1957) *The Trail of the Black Walnut:* McClelland and Stewart, Publishers, Toronto.

Chapter 2

The Emergence of an American
Wagon in Colonial Pennsylvania

T HE Conestoga wagon undoubtedly had its origin in southeastern
Pennsylvania in the early or middle part of the eighteenth
century, but details about it are lost in the mists of the past. It is unlikely that a "first" Conestoga ever was made. A variety of wagons of
sophisticated design were in use in England and central Europe by
1700, and knowledge about making such wagons came to America
with the early English and German people who settled the rich lands
lying north and west of Philadelphia. Probably some of the earliest
settlers brought farm wagons with them. At any rate, a need for
wagons developed as settlements spread farther and farther from
Philadelphia. Wagons were needed to haul farm produce to Philadelphia, and they were needed to carry the articles of civilization
from Philadelphia to the outlying settlements. Additionally, an extensive fur trade was carried on in Pennsylvania in the early part of
the eighteenth century, and wagons were used wherever roads existed
to haul furs into Philadelphia for export to Europe, and to haul the
trade goods from the city to the frontiers.

The Conestoga wagon undoubtedly took its name from the Conestoga River Valley of Lancaster County, Pennsylvania. Lancaster
County, which was settled in the early part of the eighteenth century,
lies at a minimum distance of about 45 miles from Philadelphia, and
the town of Lancaster is about 60 miles away from the city. In the
early eighteenth century it would have taken four days to make the
trip from Lancaster town to Philadelphia by wagon, so that there
was need for a cloth cover to keep rain off of perishable farm produce, and off of merchandise too. It is probable that, at some time
during the first half of the eighteenth century, people of Lancaster
County began to produce a wagon with standardized features and
details which especially suited both their needs, and their taste for
appearance. This soon became known as the *Conestoga wagon*. It is
probable, also that this early Conestoga wagon had a close resem-

blance to the smaller Conestogas of the nineteenth century which we know from surviving specimens. Unfortunately, no surviving Conestoga wagon can be associated, definitely, with a date prior to 1800, and the writers know of no eighteenth century painting or drawing showing such a wagon in detail.

English farm wagons of the eighteenth and nineteenth centuries differ in many respects from the Conestoga. In a recently published book entitled *The English Farm Wagon, Origins and Structure*, J. Geraint Jenkens discusses and illustrates the considerable variation in structure and ornamentation possessed by these wagons[1]. In contrast to the Conestoga wagon, which was widely used in a standardized form for a century or more, the English wagons differ markedly from county to county, and even from town to town and vale to vale. The running gear, or undercarriage, of English wagons usually are equipped with paired shafts instead of a single draught pole, or tongue, when horses are used. The draught pole is used when the pulling is done by oxen. The wheels of English farm wagons usually are of heavier construction than Conestoga wheels. Felloes are considerably heavier and wider. By American standards a tire four inches across is considered to be wide whereas the tires of English wagons may be as much as seven inches wide. English wheels frequently are held together with five or six iron strakes instead of with a single iron hoop. The beds of English wagons are constructed with many variations, and some have a marked curvature in the bottom rail and floor as well as in the top rail. Jenkens expresses the opinion that the Conestoga wagon was evolved by combining features of eighteenth century road wagons of England and the large wagons of western Germany.

The earliest known use of a wagon for hauling goods between Philadelphia and the land of Conestoga (or Conestogoe, as it was then written) was in the year 1716. Entries concerning this wagon, and in subsequent years, other wagons and the goods that they hauled, appear in an account book and a ledger of the Philadelphia fur merchant and trader, James Logan. These accounts also contain the first recorded use of the term "Conestogoe Waggon". Evelyn A. Benson, historian of Lancaster, has made a study of James Logan and his many activities, and it is she who brought to light these important early entries of wagoning, in a paper of the Lancaster County Historical Society[2]. The background information and entries which follow are taken from Mrs. Benson's paper. The original sources are *James Logan's Account Book 1712-1719* and *James Logan's Ledger 1720-1727,* unpublished documents in the library of the Historical Society of Pennsylvania.

James Logan was William Penn's business representative in Pennsylvania, and he was in charge of collecting money due Penn in the colony and also of selling land while Penn was alive. After Penn's death, the estate was involved in litigations and Logan continued in charge of land sales. Logan was heavily involved in carrying on the trade with the Indians, and of necessity became an able diplomat who strove to maintain peace with the Indians and to treat them fairly.

In the decade before 1715 a busy fur trade was carried on with the Conestoga Indians, with furs and skins being exchanged for imported articles brought by ship to Philadelphia. At that time pack horses were the only means of transportation. In 1705, at an Indian treaty held at Conestoga by Logan, the possibility of building a trading house there was discussed. By 1716 it had become possible for a wagon to make the trip from Philadelphia to Conestoga, and Logan's account book contains a notation for May 19, 1716 that John Miller used his wagon to bring down furs for James Patterson, Ann Le Tort, Peter Bezaillion and Martin Chartier and took back lead, gunpowder, blue duffels, rum, kettles, and salt to trade for more furs. The people mentioned were the traders who dealt with the Indians, and their names frequently appear in the account books. An entry for September, 1716 shows that John Miller, "the Wagonar", bought from Logan two half faggots of steel.

Apparently only one wagon was in use in 1716, for the accounts refer to it as "the wagon" and to payments for carriage to "Jno. Millar of Conestogoe." Other notations in 1716 and 1717 refer to goods brought down by pack horse, seven to nine horse-loads at a time. Then on May 27, 1717, a sum was paid to James Hendricks of Conestoga for goods carried "pr his Waggon" and another sum for goods which came "pr Millars Waggon," so a second wagon had been put to work. In July a third wagon, belonging to Joseph Cloud, brought in skins.

By November, 1717, James Logan had established a store house at Conestoga to sell hardware and household goods both to the German settlers and to the Indians, and he had procured a wagon for himself. On 31 December he bought what is recorded as a "Conestogoe Waggon" (FIG. 32). The entries are as follows:

18 Nov. 1717
    "Sundry Acc. Dr. Conestogoe Store House & Waggon.
    Dr. pd. Jno Ball for his Grey Stallion   £ 8.10
20 Nov. 1717
    "Conestogoe Store & Waggon Dr. to Sundry Acco. for
    Sundries sent John Cartlidge by John Balls Cart
31 Dec. 1717
    "Sundry Accot. Dr. to James Hendricks of Conestogoe
    viz. Conestogoe Waggon & Store Dr. £22 for his Wag-
    gon & a Thill horse bought of him for that money."

The fact that a thill horse was sold with the wagon strongly suggests that this first Conestoga wagon was equipped with shafts, in the
traditional English method, for *thill* is another word for the shaft of
a wagon or carriage.

Six months later the account books contain the entries:

10 June, 1718
    "Conestogoe Waggon Dr. pd. for 2 Bells 11/6 E. Jenks
    help 12s C. Jones 12
    "John Cartlidge . . . sundries sent him by my Waggon
    at his request . . . To Waggon for carriage of 1100 lb.
    at 3s   £ 1.13
    "Acct. of Merch. at Conestogoe to Sundry Accots for
    the following Goods Sent up by my Waggon viz. to
    Accot of Cargoe from Bristol."

Following this last entry is a list of goods, apparently sent to stock the
store at Conestoga: locks, gimlets, iron handsaws, steel handsaws,
hammers, spurs, augers, girths, broad axes, strap hinges, chisels,
gouges, files, silk crepe, Indian camlets, thread, tape, thimbles, pins,
needles, whip cord, children's hose, shoe buckles, hunting saddle with
snaffle bridle, shares and coulters, nails, cross cut saws, and bed cords.
On 1 July, 1718, Logan bought for the wagon twenty yards of Luback canvas for 18 pence per yard, and a larger piece of the same
material for Alexander Arbuthnot for two pounds ten shillings. Inasmuch as Miller bought the canvas for his wagon, it is probable that
he intended to use it over bows, as a cover to protect the goods he transported. A large wagon requires about twenty yards of material for
such a cover.

On the following day James Logan sent to John Cartlidge, the merchant at Conestoga, "the following Goods by my Waggon": camlet, drugget, shalloons, duroy, buttons, silk, mens stockens, silver knives and forks, iron knives and forks, horn combs, gartering, Japand Tobacco boxes, ground ginger, iron, glasses, mohair, womens fine hose, pepper, nutmeg, spices, cinnamon, cloves, mace, rum, molasses & sugar, earthenware 6 3 pt. mugs, 12 1 qt. mugs, 18 pints, 24 ½ pints, 2 chamber pots, 2 4 gal. jugs, paper, 1 1 qt. tin pot & 1 half pint ditto, 1 half gall Tin pott, a trunk & cord.

An entry of 18 September, 1718 shows a payment of £1.15.5 to Geo. Gray's wife in full payment for ferriage for the wagon. John Comb and Peter Cock received payment that year as wagoners on Logan's wagon, which made trips to the mill as well as to Philadelphia. In the winter of 1818 Logan paid twelve shillings for two new axletrees, nine shillings eight pence for eight nights' pasturage, and other amounts for hay, corn, leather, and "oyl". There also was an expenditure of eighteen pounds for "keeping six horses this winter."

Logan sold his store in Conestoga to John Cartlidge in 1726 for thirty pounds, but he retained the wagon and horses, and paid Cartlidge to keep them at his house. Logan's ledger contains an "Account of my Waggon & Team 1720-23," and this includes an "Accot of Stock for sd Waggon 6 horses & harness" at a cost of eighty-four pounds. An entry dated 19 November, 1720, is for "New forewheels to ye old wagn." During the same year Logan paid "Thomas Peel my Waggoner 1 years wages £20," and made other payments for "Peel's disbursements on his Journeys to Conestoga" for stops along the road at the houses of Thomas Moore, Castener on Pecquea Creek, Richard Hughs, Richard Lewis, Simeon Woodrow, and David Harry. In 1722 Logan's wagon and team of six horses was sold to the governor, Sir William Keith, for eighty pounds.

Thus it is established that by 1720 horse-drawn wagons were in use for carrying merchandise from Philadelphia to Lancaster County, and for carrying furs down to Philadelphia. In the next thirty years settlers from Germany, chiefly, poured into Lancaster County and into the other counties south and east of the mountains. They established farms throughout the countryside and had wagons built for themselves. It was during this period, apparently, that a more or less standardized wagon developed, and became a common, if not necessary, piece of farm equipment. These wagons soon were referred to as "Conestoga" wagons, or "Dutch" wagons.

Benjamin Franklin commented on hemp grown in Conestoga in 1747:[3] "The greater part of our hemp is brought from Conestoga, a large and very rich tract of land on the banks of the Susquehanna. It is brought down in wagons."

The February 5, 1750 issue of the Pennsylvania Gazette, a Philadelphia newspaper carried an advertisement which said, in part: "Just imported, and to be sold very cheap for ready money, by Thomas White at his house in Market Street, between 4th and 5th almost opposite the sign of the Conestoga Waggon . . . " A week later the same advertiser used the term "Dutch Waggon" in a similar advertisement.

By 1755 difficulties between England and France had reached the point of war, and England set about to eliminate the French threats to her colonies. General Braddock landed in Virginia with about 1400 regular troops and began preparing for the march against Fort Duquesne. His baggage and supply requirements could not be handled by the few wagons brought with his troops, so with the assistance of Benjamin Franklin he managed to hire more than one hundred fifty of Pennsylvania farm wagons together with teams and drivers. The story of these wagons, and their ultimate destruction, is told separately in the next chapter. From the surviving records relating to the use of these wagons by Braddock, it is apparent that at that time farm wagons were in common use in York County and the other settled lands lying west of the Susquehanna and south of the mountains.

By the time that the Revolutionary War broke out in 1775 much of the land of southeastern Pennsylvania lying south of the mountains had been settled for a couple of generations, and east of the Susquehanna for fifty or sixty years. Farms, roads, and towns were scattered throughout the region, but it was sparsely peopled by present standards. A majority of the settlers were of Germanic origin, but Englishmen were present in large numbers also. These Pennsylvania Deutsch, or Dutch as they soon were called, brought with them from Europe strong traditions of a hand-craft culture. The general peace and prosperity which these early peoples enjoyed made it possible for them to develop in Pennsylvania a hand-craft culture unequaled in post-Columbian America. The stone houses and well-built barns, the beautiful longrifles, the fractur paintings, the furniture, and the artistic ironwork from this region are famous. The Conestoga wagon, too, is the product of these peoples in these times.

Pennsylvania supplied most of the wagons used by the American army in the Revolutionary War. President Reed of the Second Provincial Congress wrote to General Washington in 1780 that "the army had been chiefly supplied with horses and wagons from this State [Pennsylvania] during the war," and mentioned that it was said that half the supplies furnished the army also came from there.[4] Conestogas carried supplies to the needy American army during the hard winter at Valley Forge. Mr. Nevin W. Moyer of Linglestown, Pa., stated in about 1929 that his great-great-great-great-grandfather, Valentine Moyer, was master of the wagon train, and his son Philip one of the wagoners.[4] Because these men knew the country between Philadelphia and Valley Forge so well, they were able to evade the redcoats and get their supplies safely to the suffering army. Philip Moyer became an officer before the end of the war, and after his death his body was carried to its final resting place. In 1923 the D.A.R. erected a stone there in his memory.

In the spring of 1778 a wagon drawn by four horses and accompanied by a full company of Continental soldiers for a guard, brought six hundred thousand dollars in silver, a loan from the French government, to the Government Treasury in York, Pennsylvania, from Portsmouth, New Hampshire.[5]

In George Washington's diary, under the date of May 17, 1775, is the entry:[6] "din'd at Mr. Sam'l Griffins. After wch attended a Commee at the Conestoga Wagon." The Conestoga Wagon Inn was located on Market Street, Philadelphia, and is the same establishment mentioned in the Pennsylvania Gazette advertisement of 1750. In 1783 a record was made of Major General Lee dying "in a small dirty room in the Philadelphia tavern called the Canastoe Wagon, designed chiefly for the entertainment and accommodation of common countrymen."[7]

During the 1780's Washington's diaries mention wagons a number of times, but they are simply referred to as wagons, no mention being made of the word "Conestoga". His entry for 28 September, 1781 is: "Having debarked all the Troops and their Baggage, marched and encamped them in front of the city [Williamsburg, Va.], and having with some difficulty obtained horses and Waggons sufficient to move our field artillery, Intrenching Tools and such other articles as were indispensibly necessary, we commenced our March for the Investiture of the Enemy at York." After 1785 his diary contains a number of entries concerning the use of wagons on his plantations.

In 1782 Schoepf wrote about the market in Philadelphia, and mentioned:[8] "The most distant, especially German country people come to the city with large covered wagons, laden with all sorts of provisions, bringing with them, at the same time, their own victuals, and feed for their horses, while remaining here."

Dr. Benjamin Rush, writing in 1789 said:[9] "A large strong waggon, covered with a linen cloth, is an essential part of the furniture of a German farm. In this waggon, drawn by four or five large horses of a peculiar breed, they convey to market over the roughest roads, two or three thousand pounds weight of the produce of their farms. In the months of September and October it is not uncommon to meet in one day from fifty to an hundred of these waggons on their way to Philadelphia, most of which belong to German farmers."

By the Treaty of Paris, at the end of the Revolutionary War, England ceded to the newly formed United States the lands of the Ohio Valley, and the land there was opened to settlement. Within a few years Pittsburgh and Wheeling became the all-important towns through which most emigrants passed on their way to the lands further west. They also were the all-important terminals where freight hauled overland by Conestoga wagon was transferred to boats for shipment on down the river to the west.

Pittsburgh had a head start on Wheeling in development, and by 1786 it was a bustling frontier town containing a good many houses, a number of stores, and boat yards hurriedly making keel boats and "Kentucke boats." A newspaper, the *Pittsburgh Gazette,* was started that year, and in it a number of items relating to wagoning are to be found. Some contemporary thoughts about the town and its future were put down in the issue for Saturday, August 26, 1786:
"OBSERVATIONS on the COUNTRY at the Head of the Ohio River with Digressions on various Subjects

"The bulk of the inhabitants [of Pittsburgh] are traders, mechanics, and laborers. Of mechanics and laborers there is still a great want. Masons and carpenters are especially wanted; indeed, from this circumstance, the improvement of the town in buildings is greatly retarded.

"This town must in future time, be a place of great manufactory. Indeed the greatest on the continent, or perhaps in the world. The present carriage from Philadelphia is five-pence for each pound of weight, and however improved the conveyance may be, and by whatever channel, yet such is our distance from either of the oceans, that the importation of heavy articles will be expensive. The manufacturing of them will therefore become more an object here than elsewhere. It is a prospect of this, with men of reflection, which renders the soil of this place so valuable."

Although the wagon road over the mountains from Philadelphia to Pittsburgh was hardly better than passable at this early date, the Conestoga freighters rolled in, carrying an incredible variety of merchandise. Hard cash was in short supply in western Pennsylvania at this time, so the merchants of Pittsburgh readily accepted a number of kinds of country produce in trade for the imported goods. Advertisements in the *Pittsburgh Gazette* frequently begin with the line "Just received from Philadelphia, and to be sold by . . . " In the issue for September 2, 1786 Wilson and Wallace list 75 kinds of merchandise from Philadelphia for sale, and include carpenters and wheelwrights axes, and waggoners tools.

Advertisements for the years 1786 and 1787 always mention Philadelphia as the source of the imported goods, if they mention a source at all, but by 1788 imports from Baltimore also are specifically mentioned. The following advertisement from the *Pittsburgh Gazette* for August 2, 1788 points out the great variety of goods that were brought in by wagon:

"Just imported in the latest vessels from Europe to Baltimore and George Town, and now opening in Pittsburgh, a large and General Assortment of EUROPEAN and WEST-INDIA GOODS, which will be sold on the lowest terms, wholesale and retail, by

Elliot, Williams, and Company

At their store the corner of Front and Ferry Streets, lately occupied by Mr. Devereux Smith

DRY GOODS, HARDWARE, and CUTLERY

Blue, green, olive claret, mixed, drab 7-8
dussins

Blue, green, scarlet, claret, brown, bottle
green, mixed, drab 6-4 broad cloths

Womens scarlet cardinals

Blue, green pink, drab, and brown cambles

Blue, green, yellow, pink, brown and white
calimancoes

Blue, green, brown, drab and white shalloons

Blue, green, crimson and pink moreens

Blue, green, brown and drab entaloons

Pink, green, blue and drab joans spinning

Jeans and sustains of different qualities

Nankeens

Corduroys, velvets, and velverets of different kinds

Buff laceinet

Cotton ribband do

Chintzes, calicoes and printed linens of
all widths and prices

German canabrigs and ticklenburghs

Barcelona black and figured silk linens
and cotton handkerchiefs

Silk, thread, cotton and worsted mens
and womens hose

Black and white flowered, figured and
plain gauze

Figured and plain muslin

Book and jaconet muslin

Plain and sprigged lawns

Flowered and needle worked lawn aprons

Blankets of all kinds and qualities

Black silk and thread laces

Sewing silk of different kinds

White and colored thread

Tully and lettered gartering

Quality binding

Checks of all kinds

Mens fine and coarse hats

Children's do

Womens beaver [hats]

Mens & Womens silk thread & leather
gloves and mitts

Mens boots and shoes

Childrens shoes

Elegant sang

Umbrellas

Double gilt coat and waist coat buttons

Baker, mohair & metal buttons

Leather, brass & Japan . . . ink pots

Sealing wax and wafers

Writing paper and quills

Powder bags and puffs

Hair powder and perma.

Shaving boxes & brushes

Dressing and looking glasses

Barbers dressing combs

Ivory and ridding do

Womens crooked do

Tooth brushes

Clothes do

Sweeping do

Shoe & buckle do

Black ball

Ostrich feathers

Foxtail do

Curry combs & brushes

Snuff in boxes

Playing cards

Wool & cotton cards

Cotton in bags

Tumblers & wine glasses

Carpenters & shoemakers tools well assorted

Knives and forks

Desert do

Carving do

Butchers do

Pen do

Pocket do

Womens & taylors scissars & shears

Ditto thimbles

Razors with strops complete

Pinchbeck, brass plated shoe and knee
buckles

Cork screws

Gimblets of all sizes

Plated and steel spurs
Sawmill, cross cut and whip saws
Steel plated and common hand do
Surveyors compasses
Smoothing irons
Candle sticks and snuffers
Hair pins
Assorted watch chains and seals
Hooks and eyes
White Chapel needles
Needles and pins
Knitting needles
Brass curtain rings
Spectacles
Money scales
Scythes and sickles

Frying pans
Gridirons
Saddles and bridles
Stirrup irons
Locks and hinges of all kinds
Brass cocks
Jews harps
Pewter dishes, plates, basons, and mugs
   of different sizes
Tin kettles
Tea cups and saucers
Crowley's steel
Bar iron
Nails of all kinds
Gunpowder, shot and bar lead
Flints

GROCERIES

Best hyson tea
Souchong and bohes do
Coffee
Chocolate
Loaf sugar
Muscovado do
Molasses
Pepper
Alspice

Nutmeg
Cinnamon
Mace
Cloves
Almonds
Raisins
Prunes
Figs
Madder

Red wood
Castile soap
Madeira, Claret, Port
   and Lisbon wines
Jamaica spirits
West India rum
Shrub and
Porter

They will receive in payment for any of the above articles cash, ginseng, peltry, bacon, beef cattle on foot, whiskey, flour, butter, cheese, tallow, candle wick, hand soap, and vinegar.

Pittsburgh July 18, 1788"

Thus the Conestoga wagon was born. Her first uses were for carrying farm produce and freight from the prosperous agricultural region south of the mountains to Philadelphia and Baltimore. But when roads to Pittsburgh, Wheeling, and the Ohio Valley were opened she came into her greater glory as the important and only practical means of bringing the articles of civilization to the peoples of the west. In the decades following the Revolutionary War slow but continued improvement was made in the condition of the roads across the mountains, and it became practical to increase the size of the wagons. These larger vehicles probably were not made before about 1810. After the War of 1812 was settled, in 1815, the classic period of Conestoga wagoning began. It lasted about thirty years, then ended rather suddenly when the railroads reached Pittsburgh and Wheeling.

REFERENCES—

1. Jenkens, J. Geraint (1961) *The English Farm Wagon, Origins and Structures:* The Oakwood Press, Tandridge La., Lingfield, Surrey.
2. Benson, Evelyn A. (1953) "The Earliest Use of the Term 'Conestoga Wagon' ": Papers of the Lancaster County [Pa.] Historical Society, v. LVII, no. 5.
3. Anonymous (1963) "East Hempfield Township": Papers of the Lancaster County [Pa.] Historical Society, v. 67, no. 1.
4. Omwake, John (1930) *The Conestoga Six-Horse Bell Teams of Eastern Pennsylvania:* John Omwake, Pub., Cincinnati.
5. Prowell, G. H. (1907) *History of York County, Pennsylvania:* J. H. Beers & Co., Chicago.
6. Fitzpatrick, John C. (1925) *The Diaries of George Washington:* Houghton Mifflin Co., New York.
7. Thornton, Richard H. (1912) *An American Glossary:*
8. Schoepf, Johann David (1911) *Travels in the Confederation, 1783-84:* translated from the German, and edited by Alfred J. Morrison, Philadelphia.
9. Rush, Dr. Benjamin (1910) *An Account of the Manners of the German Inhabitants of Pennsylvania:* Pennsylvania-German Society, Lancaster, Pa., v. 19.

Chapter 3
General Braddock's Wagons

THE fur trade was responsible for opening the great wilderness of eastern North America to the white man. Before the seventeenth century ended, thousands of traders had paddled or tramped their way through the interior of the continent, from Hudson's Bay to the mouth of the Mississippi River, and had established numerous trading posts. The territory is immense, but it was not nearly large enough for both the British and French interests to do business without competing, and then clashing with one another. The region of the Great Lakes and the upper Mississippi Valley was generally in French control during the seventeenth, and first half of the eighteenth centuries. With British settlements along the Atlantic seaboard, and with British traders working to the north and west from their settlements, the Ohio Valley grew to be an area of much importance to both sides, though occupied by neither side.

The threat of English occupation, and settlement, of the Ohio Valley became an unwelcome reality to the French in 1749 when the Ohio Company was chartered for the purpose of trading with the Indians. The governor of Virginia assigned to the company five hundred thousand acres of land lying between the Monongahela and Kanawha rivers, and the company was required to settle at least one hundred families within the territory. Such occupation would threaten the French trade lines between the Great Lakes and the Mississippi Valley, and they became resolved to prevent it. The French advanced into the valley from the north, by building a fort at Presque Isle, now Erie, another on French Creek, and a third at the confluence of French Creek with the Allegheny. This greatly alarmed Governor Dinwiddie of Virginia, and he dispatched the young George Washington, with Christopher Gist as guide, to carry a message of protest to the French commander. The French commander's reply made it clear that he intended to hold on to the occupied territory. Washington's observations during his journey to the French forts left him convinced that additional French posts and forts would be built down the Ohio. To prevent this from happening, the Virginia authorities

FIGURE 9. The Shreiner wagon is a beautifully proportioned Conestoga farm wagon with deeply curved lines.

FIGURE 10. This large Conestoga freight wagon is owned by Earl Koons of Waynesboro, Pa., who is astride the horse. His nephew, Calvin Koons, is on the lazy board, and his grandson, Earl Ludy, is between them.
Photo by Crouse Studio, Waynesboro, Pa.

FIGURE 11. A Conestoga wagon owned by Franklin and Marshall College of Lancaster, Pa., is shown here as it appeared at the Pennsylvania Dutch Folk Festival at Kutztown in 1959. The fine team of Belgian horses is owned by Edgar Messerschmidt of Myerstown, Pa., who is shown in the wagoner's saddle.

FIGURE 12. A Conestoga wagon, with its original bows, and remnants of its original cloth cover, stands before the general store at the Shelburne Museum, Shelburne, Vt. *Shelburne Museum, Inc.*

FIGURE 13. In 1954 this large Conestoga wagon was driven from Lancaster, Pa., to Wheeling, W. Va., carrying a cargo of mail, feed grain, and tobacco. *Oglebay Institute, Wheeling, W. Va.*

FIGURE 14. A large Conestoga wagon, with eleven bows, which was driven from Lancaster, Pa., to Wheeling, W. Va., in 1954. *Oglebay Institute, Wheeling, W. Va.*

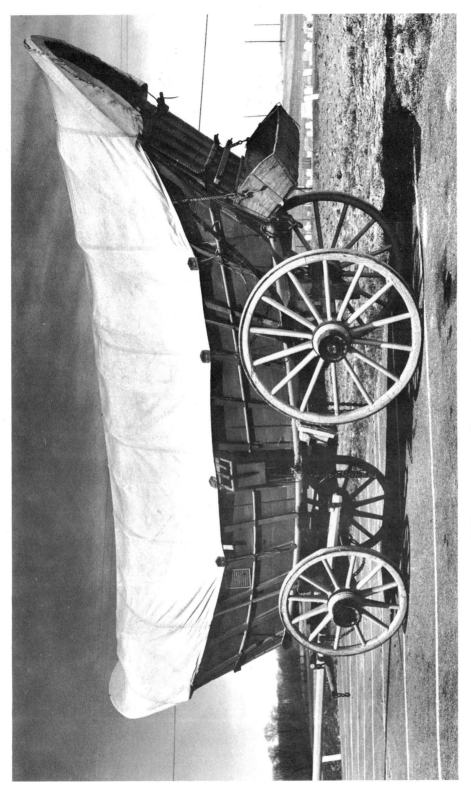

FIGURE 15. This large and well-proportioned Conestoga wagon is owned by Franklin and Marshall College in Lancaster, Pa. The overall length of the wagon box is 17 feet; the front wheels have a diameter of 48 inches; the rear wheels have a diameter of 60 inches; there are 12 bows. *N. P. Laird, Franklin and Marshall College, Lancaster, Pa.*

FIGURE 16. This particularly beautiful and graceful Conestoga wagon is in the collection of the Metropolitan Toronto Conservation Authority, Woodbridge, Ontario. *The Smithsonian Institution, Washington, D. C.*

had the Ohio Company send about forty men to build a fort at the head of the Ohio. After they had the work underway, a French force of a thousand men descended upon them and they surrendered without resistance. The English were allowed to return to Virginia, and the French completed the fort and named it Fort Duquesne. This was in the spring of 1754. Washington's unsuccessful attempt to retake the region, and his capitulation at Fort Necessity took place in the following months.

Major-General Edward Braddock was appointed commander-in-chief of the British forces in America in 1755, and he arrived in Virginia in February of that year, to carry out the war against the French. A four-pronged campaign was planned, with the intention of expelling the French from Acadia, recapturing Crown Point, taking Fort Niagara, and recapturing Fort Duquesne. The general himself was to lead the expedition against Duquesne. George Washington accepted a position on his staff as aide-de-camp, with the rank of colonel.

The trading post and settlement at Will's Creek on the upper Potomac River, at the present site of the city of Cumberland, was chosen as the point of assembly for the expedition. Braddock had about 1400 regular troops with him, and the Virginia assembly provided about 450 provincials. The general was determined to take with him all of the usual heavy baggage and provisions that normally went with such a large force of regular troops, although Washington advised him to travel lightly and to use pack horses rather than wagons.

The necessary wagons and horses were not part of the equipment which had accompanied the regular troops, and these had to be procured in the colonies. Captain Robert Orme, one of Braddock's officers, wrote in his journal[1]:

"General Braddock apprehended the greatest difficulty in procuring waggons and horses sufficient to attend him upon his march, as the Assembly had not passed an Act for supplying them, but Sir John St. Clair assured the General that the inconveniency would be easily removed, for in going to Fort Cumberland he had been informed of a great number of Dutch settlers, at a foot of the mountain called the Blue Ridge, who would undertake to carry by the hundred the provisions and stores, and that he believed he could provide otherwise two hundred waggons and fifteen hundred carrying horses to be at Fort Cumberland by the first of May."

But the wagons and horses were slow in arriving, and the General appealed to Benjamin Franklin for assistance. In his autobiography Franklin says:[2]

"We found the General at Frederictown, waiting impatiently for the return of those he had sent through the back parts of Maryland and Virginia to collect waggons. . . . When I was about to depart, the returns of the waggons to be obtained were brought in, by which it appear'd they amounted only to twenty-five, and not all of those in serviceable condition. The General and all the officers were surpris'd, declar'd the expedition was then at an end, being impossible, and exclaim'd against the ministers for ignorantly landing them in a country destitute of the means of conveying their stores, baggage, etc., not less than one hundred and fifty waggons being necessary. I happen'd to say I thought it was pity they had not landed rather in Pennsylvania, as in that country almost every farmer had his waggon. The General eagerly laid hold of my words, and said, 'Then you, sir, who are a man of interest there, can probably procure them for us; and I beg you will undertake it.' I asked what terms were to be offer'd the owners of the waggons; and I was desir'd to put on paper the terms that appeared to me necessary. This I did, and they were agreed to, and a commission and instructions accordingly prepared immediately. What those terms were will appear in the advertisement I publish'd as soon as I arriv'd at Lancaster, which being, from the great and sudden effect it produc'd, a piece of some curiosity, I shall insert it at length, as follows:"

"ADVERTISEMENT

Lancaster, April 26, 1755

"Whereas, one hundred and fifty waggons, with four horses to each waggon, and fifteen hundred saddle or pack horses, are wanted for the service of his majesty's forces now about to rendezvous at Will's Creek, and his excellency General Braddock having pleased to empower me to contract for the hire of the same, I hereby give notice that I shall attend for that purpose at Lancaster from this day till Friday evening, where I shall be ready to agree for waggons and teams, or single horses, on the following terms, viz:

1. That there shall be paid for each waggon, with four good horses and a driver, fifteen shillings per diem; and for each able horse with

a pack saddle, or other saddle and furniture, two shillings per diem; and for each able horse without a saddle, eighteen pence per diem.

2. That the pay commence from the time of their joining the forces at Will's Creek, which must be on or before the 20th of May ensuing, and that a reasonable allowance be paid over and above for the time necessary for their travelling to Will's Creek and home again after their discharge.

3. Each waggon and team, and every saddle or pack horse, is to be valued by indifferent persons chosen between me and the owner; and in case of the loss of any waggon, team, or other horse in the service, the price according to such valuation is to be allowed and paid.

4. Seven days' pay is to be advanced and paid in hand by me to the owner of each waggon and team, or horse, at the time of contracting, if required, and the remainder to be paid by General Braddock, or by the paymaster of the army, at the time of their discharge, or from time to time, as it shall be demanded.

5. No drivers of waggons, or persons taking care of the hired horses, are on any account to be called upon to do the duty of soldiers, or be otherwise employed than in conducting or taking care of their carriages or horses.

6. All oats, Indian corn, or other forage that waggons or horses bring to the camp, more than is necessary for the subsistence of the horses, is to be taken for the use of the army, and a reasonable price paid for the same.

Note.—My son, William Franklin, is empowered to enter into like contracts with any person in Cumberland county.

B. FRANKLIN."

"To the inhabitants of the Counties of Lancaster, York, and Cumberland.

"Friends and Countrymen;

"Being occasionally at the camp at Frederic a few days since, I found the general and officers extremely exasperated on account of their not being supplied with horses and carriages, which had been expected from this province, as most able to furnish them; but through the dissensions between our governor and Assembly, money had not been provided, nor any steps taken for that purpose.

"It was proposed to send an armed force immediately into these counties, to seize as many of the best carriages and horses as should be wanted, and compel as many persons into the service as would be necessary to drive and take care of them.

"I apprehend that the progress of British soldiers through these counties on such an occasion, especially considering the temper they are in, and their resentments against us, would be attended with many and great inconveniences to the inhabitants, and therefore more willingly took the trouble of trying first what might be done by fair and equitable means. The people of these back counties have lately complained to the Assembly that a sufficient currency was wanting; you have an opportunity of receiving and dividing among you a very considerable sum; for, if the service of this expedition should continue, as it is more than probable it will, for one hundred and twenty days, the hire of these waggons and horses will amount to upward of thirty thousand pounds, which will be paid you in silver and gold of the king's money.

"The service will be light and easy, for the army will scarce march above twelve miles per day, and the waggons and baggage-horses, as they carry those things that are absolutely necessary to the welfare of the army, must march with the army, and no faster; and are, for the army's sake, always placed where they can be most secure, whether in a march or in a camp.

"If you are really, as I believe you are, good and loyal subjects to his majesty, you may now do a most acceptable service, and make it easy to yourselves; for three or four of such as can not separately spare from the business of their plantations a waggon and four horses and a driver, may do it together, one furnishing the waggon, another one or two horses, and another the driver, and divide the pay proportionately between you; but if you do not this service to your king and country voluntarily, when such good pay and reasonable terms are offered to you, your loyalty will be strongly suspected. The king's business must be done; so many brave troops, come so far for your defense, must not stand idle through your backwardness to do what may be reasonably expected from you; waggons and horses must be had; violent measures will probably be used, and you will be left to seek for a recompense where you can find it, and your case, perhaps, be little pitied or regarded.

"I have no particular interest in this affair, as, except the satisfaction of endeavoring to do good, I shall have only my labor for my pains. If this method of obtaining the waggons and horses is not likely to succeed, I am obliged to send word to the general in fourteen days; and I suppose Sir John St Clair, the hussar, with a body of soldiers, will immediately enter the province for the purpose, which I shall be sorry to hear, because I am very sincerely and truly your friend and well-wisher,

B. FRANKLIN."

Good old Benjamin Franklin! The pen certainly was a mighty sword for him. The wagons, of course, began to arrive at Will's Creek. To help secure the remaining provisions that were needed, Franklin ran the following advertisement in the Pennsylvania Gazette on 22 May, 1755:

"Forty-one waggons are immediately needed, to carry each a Load of Oats and Indian Corn from Philadelphia to Will's Creek, for which they are to be paid at their Return Twelve Pounds each Waggon. Protections and Passes will be given the Waggoners by Authority of the General, to prevent their being impressed or detained after Delivery of their Loads. They are to set out together on Thursday the 29th Instant. Apply to Benjamin Franklin, in Philadelphia. Note—Several Neighbors may conveniently join in fitting out a Waggon, as was lately done in the Back Counties. If the Waggons cannot thus be obtained, there must be an impress."

After quoting this, Franklin's autobiography continues:

"I received of the general about eight hundred pounds, to be disbursed in advance-money to the waggon owners, etc.; but that sum being insufficient, I advanc'd upward of two hundred pounds more, and in two weeks the one hundred and fifty waggons, with two hundred and fifty-nine carrying horses, were on their march for the camp. The advertisement promised payment according to the valuation, in case any waggon or horse should be lost. The owners, however, alleging they did not know General Braddock, or what dependence might be had on his promise, insisted on my bond for the performance, which I accordingly gave them. . . . The general, too, was highly satisfied with my conduct in procuring him the waggons, etc., and readily paid my account of disbursements, thanking me repeatedly, and requesting my farther assistance in sending provisions after him. I undertook this also, and was busily employ'd in it till we heard of his defeat, advancing for the service of my own money, upwards of one thousand pounds sterling, of which I sent him an account. It came to his hands, luckily for me, a few days before the battle, and he return'd me immediately an order on the paymaster for the round sum of one thousand pounds, leaving the remainder to the next account. I consider this payment as good luck, having never been able to obtain that remainder, of which more hereafter."

One of the wagoners who appeared at Wills Creek ready to serve was young Daniel Morgan of Virginia, who achieved fame during the Revolutionary War as commander of the Virginia riflemen, and in the later part of the war as one of Washington's generals.[3,4] At the time that the call came to serve with Braddock he had over two years of wagoning experience behind him, and had saved enough money to purchase his own team and wagon.[5] Morgan hauled supplies from Winchester to Fort Cumberland in preparation for the expedition, and apparently after the General arrived in May all wagons, drivers, and horses within reach were impressed.[5]

The problem of having adequate roads available for the expedition had concerned Braddock from the start. Captain Orme noted the following:[1]

"General Braddock had applied to the Governor of Pennsylvania soon after his arrival in America, to open a road from that country toward the Ohio, to fall into his road to that place from Fort Cumberland, either at the great meadows, or at Yoxio Geni, that he might keep open a communication with Pennsylvania either for reinforcements or convoys . . . The Governor, through his zeal for His Majesty's service, had it carried into great forewardness in a very short time. Mr. Peters, the Secretary of Pennsylvania, who had been to inspect the road, waited upon the General at Fort Cumberland to inform him of its progress; The General desired Mr. Peters would, in conjunction with Governor Morris, make a contract in his name for a magazine of provisions, to be formed at Shippensburgh, sufficient to subsist three thousand men for three months and to be completed by the first of July . . . The General also fixed with Mr. Peters that the junction of the two roads should be at the Crow Foot of the Yoxio Geni. The waggons, Artillery and carrying horses were formed into three divisions, and the provisions disposed of in such a manner as that each division was victualized from that part of the line it covered, and a commissary was appointed to each. The waggon masters were to attend their respective divisions to proportion the goodness of the teams and to assist at every steep ascent by adding any number of horses from other wagons, till their respective divisions had passed. The waggoners were subdivided again into smaller divisions, every company having a certain number which they were to keep together however the line might be broke. . . .

"The form of the encampment differed very little from that of the march. Upon coming to the ground, the waggons were to draw up in close order in one line, the road not admitting more. . . . When the waggons were all closed up the waggon and horse masters were to assemble in some particular place their respective divisions and to give their orders to the waggoners and drovers. The horses were then turned out within the centinels, every centinel having orders not to suffer any horse to pass him.

"The detachment of six hundred men, commanded by Major Chapman, marched the thirteenth of May at daybreak, and it was night before the whole baggage had got over a mountain about two miles from the camp. The ascent and descent were almost perpendicular rock; three waggons were entirely destroyed, which were replaced from the camp, and many were extremely shattered."

The expedition's horses proved to be difficult to manage, and Captain Orme wrote of the situation thus:

"Most of the horses which brought up the train were either lost or carried home by their owners, the nature of the country making it impossible to avoid this fatal inconvenience, the whole being a continued forest for several hundred miles, without enclosures of bounds by which horses can be secured; they must be turned into the woods for their subsistence and feed upon leaves and young shoots of trees. Many projects, such as belts, hobbles, etc., were tried, but none of these were a security against the wilderness of the country and the knavery of the people we were obliged to employ; by these means we lost our horses almost as fast as we could collect them, and those which remained grew very weak, so we found ourselves every day less able to undertake the extra-ordinary march we were to perform.

"The General, to obviate as much as possible these difficulties, appointed a Waggon Master General, and under him waggon masters over every forty waggons; and horse Masters over every hundred horses, and also a drover to every seven horses; the waggon and horse masters with the drovers were to go into the woods with their respective divisions, to muster their horses every night and morning, and to make a daily report to the Waggon Master General, who was to report to the General."

Difficulties with the wagons and horses made the progress of the expedition considerably slower than the General had anticipated. Orme wrote:

"June 11th. The General called a council of war . . . in which it was agreed to send back two six-pounders, four cohorns, some powder and stores, which cleared near twenty waggons. All the King's waggons were also sent back to the fort, they being too heavy and requiring large horses for the shafts, which could not be procured; and country wagons were fitted for the powder in their stead. . . . The loads of all the waggons were to be reduced to fourteen hundred weight, seven of the most able horses were chosen for the howitzers, and five to each twelve pounder, and four to each waggon."

The first ten days of travel had carried the army ahead only about twenty four miles, to Little Meadows. Braddock, greatly discouraged, privately asked Washington's advice. Washington advised him to hasten foreward with a portion of the army, in light marching order, and to seize the fort before reinforcements could arrive from Canada. Accordingly, an advance party of twelve hundred men, ten pieces of cannon, a few wagons, and a train of pack horses went on ahead, but even their progress was slow. Scarcely more than three miles a day were covered, and Washington wrote in exasperation, "They halt to level every mole hill and to erect a bridge over every brook." A particularly difficult hill was encountered, and the problems of getting past it are described by Orme:

"Three hundred men with the miners (of whom the General had formed a company) had already been employed several days upon that hill. The General reconnoitered this mountain, and determined to set the engineers and three hundred more men at work upon it, as he thought it impassable by howitzers. He did not imagine any other road could be made, as a reconnoitering party had already been to explore the country; nevertheless, Mr. Spendlow, Lieutenant of the Seamen, a young man of great discernment and abilities, acquainted the General that in passing that mountain he had discovered a Valley which led quite round the foot of it. A party of an hundred men with an engineer was ordered to cut a road there, and an extreme good one was made in two days, which fell into the other road about a mile on the other side of the mountain."

The well known tragic end of the expedition came when Braddock's advance forces were attacked from ambush by a force of about 850 French, Canadians, and Indians, who made use of the trees and foliage to hide themselves. Braddock's regulars were thrown into disorder, most of his officers were killed or wounded, and he himself was mortally wounded. The artillery, wagons, and baggage were abandoned in the hasty retreat. Franklin wrote in his autobiography:

"The waggoners took each a horse out of his team and scamper'd; their example was immediately followed by others; so that all the waggons, provisions, artillery, and stores were left to the enemy."

The majority of the expedition's wagons had been left in the rear, with Dunbar, Daniel Morgan's wagon among them.[5] After the defeat, Braddock sent Washington back to Dunbar's Camp, about 45 miles away, to order forward wagons with provisions and hospital stores. Some of these met the retreating army at Gist's Plantation on 11 July, and then returned to Dunbar's Camp.[6] Most of the wagons and stores at Dunbar's Camp were burned to keep them from falling to the enemy, whose pursuit was anticipated. Wagoner Morgan assisted in this burning.[5] Additional information about the use of wagons on this campaign are presented in a study by Don H. Berkebile.[7]

Only a few of the wagons completed the return trip to Wills Creek. The owners of these wagons, together with the great majority of wagoners who returned without their wagons had to be compensated not only for their services, but also for their lost wagons and horses. Franklin's autobiography picks up the story at this point: "As soon as the loss of the wagons and horses was generally known, all the owners came upon me for the valuation which I had given bond to pay. Their demands gave me a great deal of trouble, my acquainting them that the money was ready in the paymaster's hands, but that orders for paying it must first be obtained from General Shirley, and my assuring them that I had apply'd to that general by letter; but, he being at a distance, an answer could not soon be receiv'd, and they must have patience, all this was not sufficient to satisfy, and some began to sue me. General Shirley at length relieved me from this terrible situation by appointing commissioners to examine the claims, and ordering payment. They amounted to near twenty thousand pounds, which to pay would have ruined me."

On 31 January, 1756, Governor Morris of Pennsylvania appointed Edward Shippen, Samuel Morris, Alexander Stedman and Samuel McCall, Jr., to "audit, liquidate, and settle" the accounts of the owners of all wagons, teams, and horses hired or destroyed in the expedition. The original document showing the settlement of these accounts was in the handwriting of Edward Shippen. In 1899 this was in the possession of Lewis Burd Walker, who felt it to be "of sufficient interest to students of American History to warrant its publication."[6] Unfortunately, less than one hundred copies were printed.

The *Wagoners Accounts* lists 194 names, most of them wagon owners who drove their own wagons. York is mentioned as the place of residence of 40 of the men, Lancaster for 2 of them, Shippensburg for 1, and Blue Rock for 1, the remainder having no specific locality mentioned. The valuation placed upon a wagon and team generally was between 40£ and 60£, but compensation ran as high as 85£ and as low as 25£. The accounts do not specify the number of horses in each team, but presumably it was four, and perhaps some of the low valuations were for two-horse teams. Horses generally were valued between 5£ and 10£, although payments of a little less than 4£ were made for one group of six horses, and Abraham Bear was credited with 16£ for a horse returned. In the account for Martin Kendrick a sum of 11 shillings 3 pence is listed for ferriage, presumably across the Susquehanna.

A typical account from this long document is that for Abraham Ferree of Lancaster, son of one of the leading Huguenots who came to Penn's Woods at an early date. A number of Ferrees were involved in gunsmithing and gunpowder making in the eighteenth century.

ABRAHAM FERREE, DR.

APRIL 30

To cash advanced [by Benjamin Franklin]	5	5	0
To 3 pcs 8-8 pd him by Mr. Scot	1	2	6
To 19 days allowed on ye death of one horse at 2-6	4	17	6
Balance	115	6	8
	£126	11	8

CR.

By appraisement of waggon and horses	85	10	0
By 51 days from Conestoga Creek to ye 9th July day of battle, at 15s	38	5	
By 10 bushels oats from hence, at 20d		16	8
By 10 nights hay for 4 horses		10	0
Driver's service, 10 days to Wills Creek	1	5	
By 5 days exp's driver back to Lancaster	1	5	
	126	11	8

The 194 names from this document are given below, together with the place of residence if it is mentioned. Although only two men are specifically mentioned as being from Lancaster, it is probable that many others were from there also. It is known that William Henry of Lancaster went along on the expedition as gunsmith, and in the accounts one William Henry is listed as a creditor to the amount of 50£ for "wagon and horses lost," but no mention is made of the location of his residence or of gunsmithing tools that were lost, assuming that this was the same man. Among the men from York are to be found a number with names that are associated with gunsmithing in York County, but none of the people mentioned are known to have been gunsmiths: John Long, George Ernst Myers, Abraham Sell, Anthony Sell, Jacob David Welchhance.

ALPHABETICAL LIST OF WAGONERS AND OTHERS MENTIONED IN THE ACCOUNTS

Ament, John	York	Bower, Michael	
Amspocker, Tobias		Bowsman, William	
Andsmanks, Henry	York	Boyle, James	
Ashebriner, Harbanus		Brenhar, Gerhart	
		Bricker, Peter	
Bard, Michael	York	Brilheart, Peter	York
Bartholomew, Thomas		Brinniman, Christian	
Bauchman, Michael		Brown, Alexander	
Bear, Abraham		Bruebaker, John	
Bear, Isaac		Buckanan, John	York
Bixler, Christian	York	Butt, Henry	York
Blythe, Benjamin			
Boggs, Andrew		Caklar, Peter	
Boggs, John		Callendar, Robert	
Bower, Henry		Carpenter, Emanuel	

Charles, Michael		
Christie, Thomas		
Christy, John		
Clay, Nicholas	York	
Clever, Henry		
Connagy, John		
Cook, James		
Craimer, Adam	York	
Crol, Philip		
Croyder, Michael		
Cushman, Isaiah		
Davataver, Michael		
Davis, Joseph		
Dielinhefer, Christopher	York	
Doner, Jacob		
Douglas, William		
Downer, Jacob		
Dreash, Frederick		
Drummond, Joshua		
Duffield, John	York	
Duffield, William	York	
Elefritz, George	York	
Emble, Leonard	York	
Ervin, Abraham		
Ferree, Abraham	Lancaster	
Foley, James		
Forster, Arthur		
Franklbarber, John		
Fry, Christopher		
Furnay, Philip	York	
Galbraith, John		
Garber, John		
Gardner, Peter	York	
Gibbs, Thomas		
Good, John		
Graaf, Sebastian		
Grove, Martin		
Hains, Jacob		
Hains, Philip		
Hair, J. Christian		
Hall, James		

Hambright, John		
Hamilton, Charles	York	
Hamilton, James		
Hammon, Jacob		
Hartman, Jacob		
Hauldiman, Jacob & Co.		
Henry, William		
Holsinger, Barnard		
Holspalm, Conrad		
Hook, Jacob	York	
Hoopes, Adam		
Hopson, John		
Houston, John	Lancaster	
Hufman, Daniel		
Hughes, Barnabas		
Hughes, Barnabas of	Shippensburg	
Hunsinger, Jacob		
Jacobs, Henry		
Jervis, Thomas		
Kamn, Michael	York	
Kar, James		
Kendrick, Martin		
Kensel, Conrad	York	
Kinkade, John		
Kinton, Thomas		
Kittera, Thomas		
Kyhn, Dr. Adam Simon		
LaFievre, Daniel		
LeFievre, Samuel		
Laird, Mathew		
Lander, Fred.		
Landers, Benjamin		
Lauman, Bernard	York	
Lawrey, Daniel		
Lawrey, James		
Lemon, Peter		
Liphart, Henry	York	
Lippart, Hans Adam		
Little, George		
Lock, Peter		
Long, Daniel	York	
Long, James		

Long, Richard		
Low, Christian	York	
McCall, Thomas	York	
McCombe, John		
McCord, John		
McKinny, Joseph		
McPherson, Robert	York	
Magee, Richard		
Mathews, James		
Miller, Jacob	York	
Miller, John		
Miller, Ludwig Solomon	York	
Mitchell, Thomas		
Moore, John		
Morrison, James		
Mummoia, Jacob		
Murrey, David		
Myer, Titter		
Myer, Vincent		
Myers, George		
Myers, George Ernst	York	
Myers, John		
Overholster, John		
Owler, Teter		
Patterson, James		
Price, Benjamin		
Rankin, James		
Redrug, Philip		
Reynolds, John		
Richardson, Charles		
Richmond, John	York	
Roan, Charles		
Rohrer, Jacob		
Rora, John		
Ross, John	Blue Rock	
Rudolph, Little Peter		
Rudyselly, Philip		
Schultz, Martin		
Schulz, Daniel		
Scott, Josia		
Scott, Samuel		

Sell, Abraham	York	
Sell, Anthony	York	
Shallas, Theobald		
Shank, George		
Shriver, Ludwig		
Shults, John		
Shultz, Peter	York	
Simson, James		
Sinclair, William		
Sleighmaker, Matthias		
Smith, John		
Smith, John, of	York	
Smith, Thomas		
Sneavely, Jacob		
Spangler, Baltazzer		
Spegat, Henry	York	
Stoder, Christian		
Stout, David		
Stover, George Michael	York	
Stuart, Moses		
Swaine, Caleb, for Bishop		
Tanner, Michael		
Tasse, Michael		
Taylor, Robert		
Thompson, John		
Tread, Peter		
Trichler, John	York	
Upright, Philip		
Waggoner, John		
Walbone, Christian		
Welch, John		
Welchhance, Jacob David	York	
Welchover, Jacob		
Wertz, Jacob	York	
Whiteman, Abraham		
Whiteman, Martin		
Wilkyns, William		
Willheim, Jacob		
Wilson, William		
Worley, Caleb		
Worley, Francis	York	
Wright, John		

Captain Orme noted that at the time wagons were needed for Braddock's expedition, "the Assembly had not passed an Act for supplying them, . . . " This was remedied in 1757 in Pennsylvania by the passage of the following act by the general assembly :[8]

AN ACT FOR REGULATING THE HIRE OF CARRIAGES TO BE EMPLOYED IN HIS MAJESTY'S SERVICE WITHIN THE INHABITED PARTS OF THIS PROVINCE.

To prevent exhorbitant demands for the hire of horses and wagons to be employed in His Majesty's service within the inhabited parts of this province and for the better supplying the same:

[SECTION I.] Be it enacted by the Honorable William Denny, Esquire, Lieutenant-Governor under the Honorable Thomas Penn and Richard Penn, Esquires, true and absolute Proprietaries of the Province of Pennsylvania and counties of Newcastle, Kent and Sussex upon Delaware, by and with the advice and consent of the representatives of the freemen of said Province in General Assembly met, and by the authority of the same, That for the better and more regular provision of carriages and horses for His Majesty's forces in their marches or for their arms, clothes or accoutrements through the inhabited parts of this province, all justices of the peace within their several counties, being duly required thereunto by an order from the governor or commander-in-chief of this province for the time being or the commanding officer of the King's forces so as aforesaid marching through the inhabited parts of this province, shall as often as such order is brought and shown unto one or more of them by some one or more of the officers of the regiment, detachment, troop or company so ordered to march issue out his or their warrants to the constables of the township from, through, near or to which such regiment, detachment, troop or company shall be ordered to march, requiring them to make provision of carriages, with able men to drive the same, as is mentioned in the said warrant, allowing them sufficient time to do the same, that the neighboring parts may not always bear the burden. And in case sufficient carriages cannot be provided within any such township [or townships], then the next justice or justices of the peace of the county shall upon such order as aforesaid being brought or shown to one or more of them by any of the officers aforesaid issue his or their warrants to the constables of such next township or county for the purpose aforesaid to make up such deficiency. And the aforesaid officer or officers who by virtue of the aforesaid warrant from the justices of the peace are to demand the carriage or carriages therein-mentioned of the constable to whom the warrant is directed, is and are hereby required at the same time to pay down in hand to the said constable for the use of the person who shall provide such carriages and men the sum of fifteen shillings *per diem* for every wagon or cart with a driver, the said driver maintaining himself and horses, the load of each wagon or cart not to exceed twenty hundredweight. And the said constable is hereby required to give a receipt in writing to the person or persons paying the same. And such constable shall order and appoint such person or persons having carriages within their respective townships, as they shall think proper, to provide and furnish such carriages, horses and men according to the warrant aforesaid, who are thereby required to provide and furnish the same accordingly. And if any military officer or officers for the use of whose troop or company the carriage was provided shall force and constrain any wagon, cart or carriage to travel more than one day's journey, or shall not discharge the same in due time for their return home, or shall suffer any soldier or servant (except such as are sick) or any woman to ride in the wagon or cart or carriage aforesaid, or shall force any constable by threatenings or menacing words to provide saddle horses for themselves or servants, or shall force horses from the owners by themselves, servants or soldiers, every such officer for every such offense shall forfeit the sum of five pounds, proof thereof being made upon oath or affirmation before two of His Majesty's justices of the peace of the same county, who are to certify the same to the paymaster of His majesty's forces within this province, who is hereby required to pay the aforesaid sum of five pounds according to the order and appointment under the hands and seals of the aforesaid justices of the peace of the same county, who are hereby empowered to deduct the same out of each officer's pay.

[Section II.] And be it further enacted by the authority aforesaid, That if any constable shall willfully neglect or refuse to execute such warrants of the justices of the peace as shall be directed unto them for providing carriages as aforesaid, or if any person or persons appointed by such constable to provide and furnish any carriage and man shall refuse or neglect to provide the same, or any other person or persons whatsoever shall willfully do any act or thing whereby the execution of the said warrants shall be hindered or frustrated, every such constable or other person or persons so offending shall for every such offense forfeit any sum not exceeding forty shillings nor less than twenty shillings to the use of the poor of the township where any such offense shall be committed, and all and every such offense shall and may be inquired of, heard and fully determined by two justices of the peace living in or near the place where such offense shall be committed, who have hereby power to cause the said penalty to be levied by distress and sale of the offender's goods and chattels, rendering the overplus if any to the owner.

[Section III.] And be it further enacted by the authority aforesaid, That every innkeeper keeping an inn or house of entertainment on any public road or roads within this province shall keep sufficient quantities of hay, oats, Indian corn or rye for the accommodation and use of the horses and creatures of such as are employed or engaged in His Majesty's service who may have occasion to pass through the inhabited parts of this province, and shall demand, have and receive according to the following rates and no more: (That is to say) for every hundred weight of good hay three shillings and six pence; for hay for each horse for one night eight pence; for oats per bushel three shillings; for Indian corn per bushel three shillings and six pence; for rye per bushel three shillings and six pence, and so in proportion for a smaller quantity of all or any of them.

And if any such innkeeper shall neglect to provide a sufficient quantity of hay, oats, Indian corn or rye as aforesaid, or shall demand more or greater prices than this act directs, he, she or they so offending shall forfeit and pay the sum of forty shillings each for every such offense, to be recovered as debts under forty shillings are directed to be recovered, one-half to the prosecutor and the other half to the overseers of the poor for the use of the poor of the city, borough or township where the same shall be recovered.

This act to continue for the space of one year and from thence to the end of the next sitting of the assembly and no longer.

> Passed March 17, 1757. Referred for consideration by the King in Council, January 27, 1758, and allowed to become a law by lapse of time in accordance with the proprietary charter.

This act expired in due time, and it was passed again on 8 April, 1758, with a new paragraph being added to Section III, and Section IV being added also:[8]

[SECTION III. (continued)] And whereas an expedition is now intended and carrying on against His Majesty's enemies to the westward of this province, in which it will be absolutely necessary that a number of carriages and horses should be procured for the transportation of provisions and other necessaries for the King's forces employed therein:

[SECTION IV.] Be it [therefore] enacted by the authority aforesaid, That the carriages and horses wanted for the said expedition shall be procured in the same manner as the other carriages and horses are hereby directed to be procured, and the said owner or owners of every carriage and four horses with a driver that shall be employed in the said expedition shall be paid by the officer demanding the same the sum of fifteen shillings *per diem* for every day he shall be so employed until he shall return to his habitation, and the driver and horses shall be maintained and supported at the charge of the Crown; and that the owner or owners of six horses with pack saddles and a driver shall have and receive twelve shillings *per diem* until he shall return to his place of abode and be maintained in like manner; and that every carriage and horse shall be valued and appraised by four indifferent persons, two whereof shall be chosen on the part of His Majesty and two on the part of the owners, before the same shall be taken into the said service; and in case any of the said carriages and horses should be lost, destroyed, killed, taken by the enemy or otherwise rendered useless to the owners, the said valuation shall be paid to the respective owner or owners of such carriages and horses that shall be so lost, destroyed, killed, taken by the enemy or otherwise rendered useless by the commander-in-chief of His Majesty's forces in these parts.

This act to continue for the space of one year and from thence to the end of the next sitting of assembly and no longer.

The expedition referred to in this act was that of General John Forbes, who marched from Philadelphia with three hundred Royal Americans, twelve hundred Highlanders, sixteen hundred Virginians, twenty-seven hundred Pennsylvanians, and a thousand wagons, to take possession of the fort at the Forks of the Ohio. In the three years since Braddock's defeat a line of forts had been established along the frontier. The Forbes expedition took the King's Highway which led from Philadelphia to Lancaster, then went on to Harris' Ferry, where a stockade had been built in 1755. From there they marched to Fort Lowther, where Carlisle is today, and then on to Fort Morris, at Shippensburgh, over the road cut in 1755 at the request of Braddock. Then they continued on to Fort Chambers, Fort Louden, Fort Lyttleton, Fort Bedford, and then to Fort Duquesne,

FIGURE 17. A relatively small but graceful nine-bow Conestoga owned by D. H. Berkebile. *The Smithsonian Institution, Washington, D. C.*

FIGURE 18. A large, well designed, and sturdily built Conestoga freighter owned by the Eleutherian Mills-Hagley Foundation. *Hagley Museum, Wilmington, Del.*

FIGURE 19. Front view of the Hagley Museum wagon. *Hagley Museum, Wilmington, Del.*

FIGURE 20. Side view of the Hagley Museum wagon. The rear wheels have a diameter of 68½ inches and the front wheels a diameter of 50 inches. Hagley Museum, Wilmington, Del.

FIGURE 21. In 1807 this wagon was driven by Abraham Weber from Lancaster County, Pa., to Waterloo County, Ontario. This is a relatively small and light wagon for farm use or for emigrant use, but the construction and ironing are basically the same as on the larger Conestogas of later date. The date of 1807 is the earliest that definitely can be ascribed to any known wagon of Conestoga construction. *Ontario Dept. Travel & Publicity, Toronto, Ontario.*

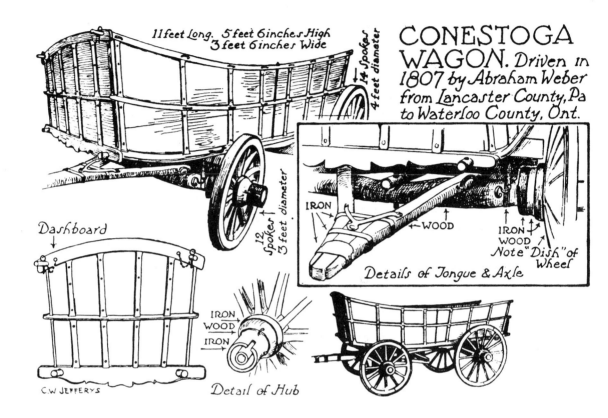

Dashboard

CONESTOGA
WAGON. Driven in
1807 by Abraham Weber
from Lancaster County, Pa
to Waterloo County, Ont.

11 feet Long. 5 feet 6 inches High
3 feet 6 inches Wide

14 Spokes
4 feet diameter

12 Spokes
3 feet diameter

IRON
←WOOD

IRON
WOOD
Note "Dish" of
Wheel

Details of Tongue & Axle

C.W. JEFFERYS

IRON
WOOD
IRON

Detail of Hub

FIGURE 22. Details of the Weber wagon. *From "The Picture Gallery of Canadian History", v. 2, by C. W. Jeffreys; Ryerson Press, Toronto, 1945.*

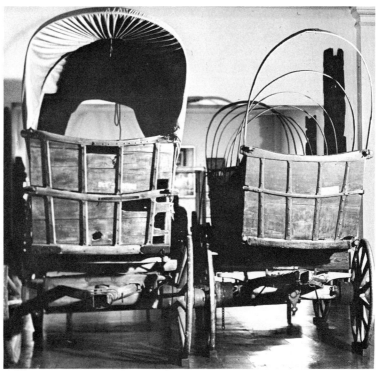

Figure 23. These two Conestogas were left to the Hershey Museum by Mr. Nevin W. Moyer of Linglestown, Pa. The wagon without the cloth cover has graceful and pleasing lines. *Photos by R. Warrington, courtesy Hershey Museum, Hershey, Pa.*

FIGURE 24. This ten-bow Conestoga wagon has dimensions which place it in the freighter or road wagon category. The box is 19 feet long overall, the rear wheels are 63 inches in diameter, and the front wheels are 47 inches in diameter. *Henry Ford Museum, Dearborn, Michigan.*

which was renamed Fort Pitt. And thus, nearly twenty years before the American Revolutionary War, the mountains had been breached with a wagon road that gave access to the waterways of the great Mississippi Valley.

The Pennsylvania assembly passed a supplementary act on 20 September, 1758, to assist General Forbes in procuring provisions.

A SUPPLEMENT TO THE ACT, ENTITLED
"AN ACT FOR REGULATING THE HIRE OF CARRIAGES
TO BE EMPLOYED IN HIS MAJESTY'S SERVICE."

Whereas by an act passed by this assembly in the thirty-first year of His Majesty's reign, entitled "An act for regulation the hire of carriages to be employed in His Majesty's service," it was amongst other things enacted that to prevent exhorbitant demands for the hire of horses and wagons to be employed in His Majesty's service, every owner or owners of every carriage and four horses with a driver employed in the present expedition against His Majesty's enemies to the westward of this province should be paid by the officer demanding the same the sum of fifteen shillings *per diem* for every day he should be so employed until he should return to his habitation, and the driver and horses should be maintained and supported at the charge of the Crown:

But forasmuch as the difficulties which have arisen in procuring a sufficient quantity of oats, straw, hay and other provisions for the horses belonging to such carts and wagons as have been hitherto employed in the said expedition beyond the inhabited parts of this province have rendered many of the horses employed therein unable to perform the service, by which and other means the army on our western frontiers under the command of General Forbes appears to be in want of a further supply of provisions to be transported from the interior parts of this province to Raystown, for remedying whereof and for the more effectual and speedy procuring a sufficient number of carriages for the transporting thereof:

[SECTION I.] Be it enacted by the Honorable William Denny, Esquire, Lieutenant-Governor under the Honorable Thomas Penn and Richard Penn, Esquires, true and absolute Proprietaries of the Province of Pennsylvania and counties of Newcastle, Kent and Sussex upon Delaware, by and with the advice and consent of the representatives of the freemen of the said Province in General Assembly met, and by the authority of the same, That from and after the publication of this act all carriages and horses wanted for His Majesty's use to be employed in the said expedition shall be procured by the act hereinbefore-mentioned until they shall arrive at their respective places of loading and shall receive their loads; and the owner or owners of every such carriage or carriages shall be paid by the officer demanding the same the sum of two and twenty shillings for every hundred weight which shall be carried or transported from the town of Lancaster to Raystown, and so from any other place or places between Lancaster and Raystown, in proportion to the respective distances except the weight of the provisions for the maintenance of the horses hereinafter provided, anything herein or in any act of this province to the contrary notwithstanding.

Provided nevertheless, That each load shall amount at least to fourteen hundred-weight for each and every carriage with four horses over and above the weight of the straw, hay, oats, or other grain for the maintenance of the horses hereinafter mentioned and provided.

And for the more speedy and effectual providing of carriages for the purposes aforesaid:

[SECTION II.] Be it further enacted by the authority aforesaid, That the owner and owners of each and every carriage employed or to be employed in transporting provisions to Raystown for the use of the army as aforesaid shall be allowed and have right to put into and load on his carriage so as aforesaid employed in His Majesty's service, at his own proper cost and charge and not to be accounted any part of his load to be paid for by the Crown, the quantity of thirty bushels of oats or a weight equal thereto in hay, straw, (rye) or any other grain for the subsistence of his or their horses respectively in their journey or journeys to Raystown and their return to their own respective habitations.

Apparently there were many broken contracts on the part of the wagoners supplying General Forbes, for nine days later, on 29 September, the assembly passed an additional act providing that those wagoners who deserted from their contract before reaching Raystown were to be fined twenty pounds.

The primary act for the hire of carriages, which expired annually, was passed again on 21 April, 1759, and again on 8 July, 1763. It was renewed for the last time on 30 May, 1764.[9]

REFERENCES—

1. Sargent, Winthrop (1855) *The History of an Expedition Against Fort DuQuesne:* Philadelphia.
2. Franklin, Benjamin (1961) *The Autobiography of Benjamin Franklin:* Washington Square Press, Inc., 630 Fifth Ave., New York.
3. Callan, North (1961) *Daniel Morgan, Ranger of the Revolution:* Holt, Rinehart and Winston, New York.
4. Higginbotham, Don (1961) *Daniel Morgan, Revolutionary Rifleman:* University of North Carolina Press, Chapel Hill, N. C.
5. Graham, James (1856) *The Life of General Daniel Morgan:* New York.
6. Walker, Lewis Burd, editor (1899) *The Burd Papers: The Settlements of the Waggoners' Accounts Relating to General Braddock's Expedition Towards Fort DuQuesne, by Edward Shippen, et al., Commissioners:* Note—less than 100 copies of this were printed—one of them is in the Library of Congress.
7. Berkebile, Don H. (1959) "Conestoga Wagons in Braddock's Campaign 1755": U. S. National Museum Bulletin 218, p. 141-153.
8. Pennsylvania, statutes (1899) *The Statutes at Large of Pennsylvania from 1682 to 1801, Vol. V, 1744 to 1759:* Pennsylvania State Printer.
9. Pennsylvania, statutes (1899) *The Statutes at Large of Pennsylvania from 1682 to 1801, Vol. VI, 1759 to 1765:* Pennsylvania State Printer.

Chapter 4
Routes, Roads, and Turnpikes

NEARLY everyone who traveled on the roads of southern Pennsylvania in the eighteenth century deplored their condition. South of the mountains, in colonial times, crude roads developed wherever there was a need for them, for the piedmont had a favorable topography that presented no barriers that could not be circumvented. But generally these were not roads in the sense that men planned and built them. They began as mere paths that people found it possible to use to get from one place to another, going first on foot, and then on horseback or with pack horse. When wagons first rolled along these trails, trees were chopped out here and there to widen the path, and troublesome boulders were pushed aside. The use of wagons continually increased and the roads became permanent. Improvements were made in the roads in the vicinity of towns, chiefly for the benefit of locals who used them most often. But the great stretches of road between towns usually were left to evolve with whatever help or hindrance indifferent nature and indifferent man would provide. As a consequence, the poor road was the common one.

By the time the French and Indian War erupted in 1755 the piedmont lands of Pennsylvania, Maryland, Virginia, and portions of the Carolinas had been settled, and wagon travel to the foot of the mountains generally was possible. Frontier settlements had been made in some of the valleys lying within the mountains, and roads leading into and along these valleys came into being. Before the war these frontier people enjoyed generally good relations with the Indians of the mountains to the north of them, but after Braddock's defeat the frontier became a bloody battleground. The border settlers lived in constant fear of attacks by raiding parties from the mountains to the north, and in many cases farms and even whole settlements were abandoned as people retreated south to more protected lands. To protect the frontier from these raids a series of forts was erected along the Pennsylvania mountain front from the Delaware River on the east to Fort Cumberland, Maryland, on the southwest.

Most of these forts were east of the Susquehanna, where most of the people were, but a few lay to the west of it, such as Granville, Shirley, Littleton, and Bedford. These western forts are important to the story of Conestoga wagoning because a number of them lay along the road that eventually was opened to Pittsburgh. During the war roads connecting these forts were opened and maintained sufficiently well that supply wagons could get to the forts.

While Braddock was making preparations for his march against Duquesne in the early spring of 1755, his deputy quartermaster-general, Sir John St. Clair wrote to Governor Morris of Pennsylvania asking that Pennsylvania "open a road toward the head of Youghheagang or any other way that is nearer the French forts," so that stores supplied by the northern colonies might go by a shorter route than that through Maryland and Virginia[1]. Morris replied " . . . there is no Waggon Road from Carlisle West through the Mountains but only a Horse Path, by which the Indian traders used to carry their Goods and Skins to and from the Ohio while that trade remained open."[2] Within a month or two, work on the road west from Carlisle was in progress under the direction of James Burd. On 12 June Allison and Maxwell wrote to Richard Peters that "Sidelong Hill [67 miles west of Carlisle and 30 miles east of Raystown] is cut very artificially, nay more so than We ever saw any; the first waggon that carried a Load up it took fifteen Hundred without even stopping; . . . for four Days the Labourers had not one Glass of Liquor!"[3] Certain hardships, such as a scarcity of liquor, had to be endured in time of war. On 15 June the road was cleared to Raystown, now known as Bedford.[4] There were uncertainties about the route for the road west of Raystown, although it was understood that it probably would go through Turkey Foot, also called Three Forks, on the Youghiogheny River. Before the road progressed more than a few miles west of Raystown, Braddock was routed and the road-building party retired to Fort Cumberland for safety.

The remainder of 1755 was a dark time for the frontier settlements of Pennsylvania and Virginia. Indian raids were numerous then, and also in the spring and summer of 1756, after a winter of quiet. Late in 1756 the Pennsylvania Assembly took positive action by authorizing the construction of a chain of forts along the Blue Mountains, from the Delaware to the Potomac. Particular attention was paid to the forts at Carlisle, Shippensburg, Louden, and Lyttleton, because they were on the projected road to the west. After these forts were secure, an important step toward Duquesne was taken by the establishment of a fort at Raystown (Bedford) in 1757.

The American war campaigns planned for 1758 involved an attack on Louisburg, a push up Lake Champlain, and an expedition against Fort Duquesne. Brigadier John Forbes was chosen to head the campaign against Duquesne, and an army of more than six thousand eventually was assembled. Raystown was chosen as a base of operations and point of assembly for the army, and the original plan was to cut a road down to Fort Cumberland and then to move against Duquesne by means of Braddock's Road. It was realized, however, that if a new road were cut directly across the country to Duquesne, it would be considerably shorter than the route through Cumberland. Throughout the spring and summer of 1758, while the army was assembling and preparing to march, the problem of whether to use the old road or to cut a new one was argued and discussed between Forbes, his quartermaster-general, Sir John St. Clair, his assistant, Lt. Col. Henry Bouquet, and George Washington, in charge of the Virginia troops. Washington argued in favor of the route through Ft. Cumberland and along Braddock's Road. After weighing the many arguments for and against each of the routes, Forbes at last decided on cutting the new road, and work on it began on August 1.

By 23 August wagons were over Allegheny Mountain and at Stoney Creek, and in early September an advance party of 1500 men were at an advanced post about forty miles from Ft. Duquesne. But road building went slowly, and was further slowed by heavy fall rains. By early November the whole army was in the vicinity of Ligonier, discouraged by the thoughts of approaching winter. But then word came that the French had abandoned Ft. Duquesne, and the army pushed ahead with renewed strength. By 25 November the army was in possession of the remains of the fort, and a couple of days later General Forbes wrote a letter to Pitt, the British Secretary of State, under the heading "Pittsborough 27th Novemr 1758."[4]

Forbes' Road was kept open, and used as a military supply road until the war ended in 1763. Whether or not it remained open as a usable wagon road from then until the Revolutionary War began is not known. A. B. Hulbert, who wrote a detailed account of the building of the road and the planning that preceded it, stated that the road was kept open in the time between the two wars, and used as a supply road during the Revolution.[4] Other evidence suggests that the road reverted to a pack horse trail for a number of years.[5] No matter which situation is true, the road definitely was open as a wagon road by 1783, and by that time was known as the Pennsylvania Road.

Southwestern Pennsylvania and the adjacent parts of present West Virginia were settled mainly in the five-year period from 1769 to 1774. By midsummer of 1771 it was estimated that there were ten thousand families in the upper Ohio country, and by 1774 it was estimated that there were fifty thousand people living west of the Allegheny Ridge and south of the Ohio and Allegheny Rivers in Pennsylvania.[6] George Croghan wrote on October 2, 1770:[6] "What number of families has settled since the congress [of Fort Stanwix], to the westward of the high ridge, I cannot pretend to say positively; but last year, I am sure, there were between four and five thousand, and all this spring and summer the roads have been lined with wagons moving to the Ohio." It is clear from this statement that by one route or another wagons were being taken over the highest ridge and into the Ohio Valley by the spring of 1770.

The main road from Philadelphia leading to Lancaster, and the western lands beyond, had its beginnings in the first two decades of the eighteenth century. Year by year an ever-increasing traffic passed back and forth along it — farmers, emigrants, freighters, military people, plus the others who traveled for business or pleasure. The road was maintained in a haphazard way, with improvements being made here and there from time to time, as required by absolute necessity. In the decade that followed the Revolutionary War this traffic became so heavy that a better road became a necessity, and plans for building a turnpike were hatched. The diary of Jacob Hiltzheimer, a member of the Pennsylvania General Assembly, had the following entry for 27 November, 1786:[7] "In the evening met seven of the members of the Assembly at a tavern opposite the State House, where we conversed about the new road to be laid out from Schuylkill to the westward, and which way the money is to be raised to make it a turnpike."

The enterprise was incorporated under the name of the Philadelphia and Lancaster Turnpike Company on 9 April, 1792. Stock was issued at $300 per share, and in a frenzy of speculation all available shares were bought in a short time. The stock certificates were printed on sheepskin, and at the top of each was a picture of the road and a

Conestoga wagon approaching a toll gate.[7] The act of incorporation states at the beginning:[8]

"Whereas the great quantity of heavy articles of the growth and produce of the country and of foreign goods which are daily transported between the city of Philadelphia and the western counties of the State requires an amendment of the highway, which can only be effected by artificial beds of stone and gravel disposed in such a manner as to prevent the wheels of carriages from cutting into the soil, the expenses whereof will be great, and it is reasonable that those who will enjoy the benefits of such highway should pay a compensation therefor, and there is reason to believe that such highway will be undertaken by an association of citizens if proper encouragement be given by the Legislature."

Much information about this turnpike to Lancaster, and about the inns and life associated with it were gathered together by J. F. Sachse and published in his book, *The Wayside Inns on the Lancaster Roadside between Philadelphia and Lancaster*.[8] He mentions that the road was laid out to start from the west side of the Schuylkill, opposite Philadelphia, and to proceed so as to pass near to or over the bridge on Brandywine Creek, near Downing'stown, and from there to Witmer's bridge, on Conestoga Creek, and then to the east end of King Street, in Lancaster (Fig. 35).

The incorporating Act provides that the company "shall cause a road to be laid out fifty feet wide, twenty-one feet whereof in breadth at least shall be bedded with wood, stone, gravel, or any other hard substance, well compacted together a sufficient depth to secure a solid foundation to the same; and the said road shall be faced with gravel or stone pounded in such manner as to secure a firm even surface, rising towards the middle by a graded arch, and so nearly level in its progress as that it shall in no place rise or fall more than will form an angle of four degrees with a horizontal line."[8]

A series of toll houses were set up at ten mile intervals and at each gate charges were made according to the following schedule:

For every score of Sheep,	1/8 dollar
For every score of Hogs,	1/8 dollar
For every score of Cattle,	1/4 dollar
For every Horse and rider, or led Horse	1/16 dollar

For every Sulkey, Chair, or Chaise with one horse
    and two wheels,   1/8   dollar

For every Chariot, Coach, Stage, Wagon, Phaeton,
    or Chaise, with 2 horses and four wheels,   1/4   dollar

For Either of the Carriages last mentioned, with four
    horses,   3/8   dollar

For every other Carriage of pleasure, under whatever
    name it may go, the like sums, according to the
    number of wheels and horses drawing the same.

For every Cart or Wagon whose wheels do not exceed
    the breadth of four inches, 1/8 dollar for each
    horse drawing the same.

For every Cart or Wagon whose wheels shall exceed
    in breadth four inches, and not exceed seven
    inches, 1/16 dollar for every horse drawing the
    same.

For every cart or wagon, the breadth of whose wheels
    shall be more than seven and not more than ten
    inches, or being of the breadth of seven inches
    shall roll more than 10 inches, five cents for every
    horse.

For every cart or wagon where the breadth of wheel
    shall be more than 12 inches two cents for every
    horse drawing the same.

Between December 1 and May 1, no wagon with four
    wheels, having less than four inches breadth of
    tire was to be loaded over 2 1/2 tons,
    From four to seven inch tire 3 1/2 tons,
    From seven to ten inch tire 5 tons.

Between December 1 and May 1, no cart with two
    wheels, having less than four inches breadth of
    tire was to be loaded over 1 1/4 tons,
    From four inches to seven inches 1 1/2 tons,
    From seven to ten inches 3 tons.

From 1 May to 1 December the wagon and cart limits were about
one half ton more. Sachse says:[8] "It was further ordered, that no cart,
wagon or carriage of burden whatsoever whose wheels shall not be
the breadth of nine inches at least, shall be drawn or pass over the

said road or any part thereof, with more than six horses, nor shall more than eight horses be attached to any carriage whatsoever, used on the said road; and if any wagon or other carriage shall be drawn along the said road by a greater number of horses, or with a greater weight, than is hereby permitted, 'one of the horses attached thereto shall be forefeited to the use of said Company to be seized and taken by any of their officers or servants, who shall be at liberty to choose which of the said horses they may think proper, excepting the shaft or wheel horse or horses.' "

The great turnpike was begun in the summer of 1792 and completed two years later, at a total cost of $464,142.31.[7] It was the first such road to be built in the United States, and proved to be financially rewarding to the stockholders of the company. In 1827 the stock paid seventy-two dollars a share in dividend. After the venture had proven to be successful, other turnpikes were erected in southern Pennsylvania, and by 1831 there were 2500 miles of these special roads in the state.[7] The city of Lancaster was a hub from which pikes radiated in all directions.

The third road of special importance to the Conestoga wagon is the National Road which connected Fort Cumberland, and Baltimore further to the southeast, with Wheeling (FIG. 33). This road had its beginnings as Braddock's Road. The Potomac River valley leads deep into the heart of the Appalachian Mountains, and made it possible for early eighteenth century settlers of Virginia and Maryland to penetrate the otherwise formidable mountains. By the time that Braddock's campaign got underway in 1755, Fort Cumberland was established as an advance post in the upper Potomac Valley, half way between Baltimore and the Ohio River. It afforded Braddock with a starting place lying closer to his goal than any other, and from the geographic point of view, was the logical place to start.

After Braddock's defeat, the road that so laboriously had been made for his army fell into disuse and within three years time was so overgrown as to be unusable. Forbes' Road became the one and only route to the Ohio Valley after 1758, and because of its importance as a military road, it was kept in more or less usable shape until the close of the French and Indian War, and probably remained open thereafter. The Ohio Valley took on such importance in the decades following the Revolution that the need developed for a second road, especially one that could better serve the southern states. Wheeling became a port of entry from the east second only to Pittsburgh, and road or no road, settlers from Virginia and Maryland began to cross the mountains and enter the land of promise at this town. Ohio gained statehood in 1802 and this further increased the desirability of having a second road to better bind together the far-flung young country.

The idea of building a national road was taken up in Washington, but the problem of financing prevented definite progress for a number of years. Eventually it was suggested that the road be financed by using proceeds from the sale of lands in Ohio, and the Enabling Act of 1802, by which Ohio became a state, stipulated that five per cent of the proceeds from the sale of Ohio land would be set aside for road construction. Ohio's constitutional convention insisted that three-fifths of these funds were to be used for roads within the state of Ohio, so only two per cent of the land sales money was available for use in building the road to Ohio. But the road surveys got started in 1806.

The National Road started at Cumberland, Maryland and ran through Uniontown, Brownsville, and Washington, Pennsylvania, and then on to Wheeling. The building progressed slowly, however. In 1811 the first construction contracts were let, and by the end of 1813 the first ten miles had been completed. Wheeling was finally reached in 1818, and after that the road was built on to the west, across Ohio, Indiana, and into Illinois. Heavy freight traffic was soon rolling over the mountains to Wheeling, and Conestoga wagons had their busiest days in the two decades that followed the completion of the road to Wheeling.

The story of the National Road is told in detail in a book by Philip D. Jordan, and much of the above information is taken from this source.[9] In a chapter about Conestoga wagoning on the road to Wheeling, Jordan quotes an Ohio congressman who said that a mercantile house in Wheeling in 1822 had "consigned to it 1081 wagons, loaden with merchandise, averaging about 3500 pounds each, the carriage of which amounted to $90,000. There are, besides this house, five other commission stores in Wheeling; estimating that each of these received two-thirds of the quantity of goods consigned to the other, it shews that 4681 wagons of merchandise were received at that town ... This number, at the rate of $90,000 for 1081 loads, gives for the cost of transporting merchandise from Baltimore to Wheeling, the sum of $390,000 during one year. Besides this, it is estimated that every tenth wagon at least passes through that town to the West without unloading at all, which would considerably increase the estimate." The congressman mentioned that wagoners usually carried return loads of country produce such as flour, whiskey, hemp, and tobacco, and that the making of the Cumberland Road reduced the cost of carriage to Wheeling by half.

Jordan managed to locate many specific facts relating to the freighting business along the National Road in the period after 1820 when traffic was heaviest. He mentions that Jonathan Knight stated in 1831 that it took a wagoner about 15 days, averaging 18 miles a day, to travel the 266 miles from Wheeling to Baltimore.[10] Jordan tells of a journey by Daniel Barcus, a wagoner hired to haul merchandise from Baltimore to Mt. Vernon, Ohio. He carried 8,300 pounds at $4.25 per hundred pounds, and covered 397 miles in 30 days. At Mt. Vernon he back-loaded with 7,200 pounds of Ohio tobacco which he carried at $2.75 per hundred pounds. His total income was $550.75, but from this he had to pay his traveling expenses and make his repairs, so his net was roughly $500. This sum is converted into mid-twentieth century dollars by multiplying by a factor of 6 or 8.

One additional wagon road deserves special attention because of its importance in tying together the piedmont lands from Pennsylvania to North Carolina. This was known as the Great Wagon Road, and it ran from Philadelphia through Lancaster, York, and Frederick, Maryland, to Winchester, Virginia and then continued down the Valley of Virginia to end in the vicinity of the Yadkin River in North Carolina. This route apparently was open in the middle of the eighteenth century and used by emigrants from Pennsylvania who settled in the Carolina piedmont.

Railroads were largely responsible for bringing an end to long distance wagon freighting in the middle of the nineteenth century, although the eventual industrial development of the Ohio and Mississippi Valleys lessened the dependence of the western region on the goods from Philadelphia and Baltimore. In 1828 the Columbia Railroad was laid out and begun, running westward from Philadelphia to Lancaster and then on to Columbia at the edge of the Susquehanna.[8] It was not finished until 1834. In these early years the cars were pulled by horses. An engraving in a publication of 1843 shows one of the early steam engines on a track which crossed North Queen Street in Lancaster, and in the background is a Conestoga wagon

(FIG. 30). The Baltimore and Ohio Railroad was incorporated in 1827, with the intention of building a line to connect Baltimore with Wheeling. It progressed slowly, connecting first to Frederick, Maryland, and then to Cumberland, and finally in 1853 it reached Wheeling. A combination of canals and railroads connected Philadelphia to Pittsburgh by 1840, and about a decade later the rail connection was complete all the way.

REFERENCES—

1. Pennsylvania, *Colonial Records,* v. vi, p. 300.
2. Pennsylvania, *Colonial Records,* v. vi, p. 302.
3. Pennsylvania, *Colonial Records,* v. vi, p. 434-435.
4. Hulbert, Archer Butler (1903) *The Old Glades (Forbes's) Road:* The Arthur H. Clark Co., Cleveland, Ohio.
5. Dunbar, Seymour (1915) *History of Travel in America:* The Bobbs-Merrill Co., Indianapolis.
6. Buck, Solon J., and E. H. Buck (1939) *The Planting of Civilization in Western Pennsylvania:* University of Pittsburgh Press.
7. Faris, John T. (1927) *Old Trails and Roads in Penn's Land:* J. B. Lippincott Co., Philadelphia.
8. Sachse, Julius F. (1912) *The Wayside Inns on the Lancaster Roadside between Philadelphia and Lancaster:* J. F. Sachse, Lancaster, Pa.
9. Jordan, Philip D. (1948) *The National Road:* The Bobbs-Merrill Co., Indianapolis.
10. Ringwalt, J. L. (1888) *Development of Transportation Systems in the United States:* Philadelphia. Quoted by P. D. Jordan (1948).

Chapter 5
Accounts of Travel on the Road

NOTHING equals a good contemporary account of travel to give the flavor and feeling of it to the reader at a later time in history. The rough and ready men who drove the wagons were not the type to record the seemingly unimportant details of their everyday life on the road. This is unfortunate, but understandable. Indeed, everyday life almost always has gone unrecorded in history, and it is only when viewed by someone from a slightly (or greatly) different culture that it is likely to be noticed at all, and described in written words. Thus some of the most informative accounts we have about travel on the roads of Conestoga land come from travelers from afar. Europeans, particularly, found American life so different from life in their own part of the world that their writings are apt to contain details that an American would overlook.

In 1778 Elizabeth Drinker[1] made the trip from Philadelphia to Lancaster, a distance of about 62 miles. This was before the building of the Lancaster Turnpike, and she wrote in her diary:

"In our journey today we found the roads so bad, that we walked part of ye way, and climbed 3 fences, to get clear of ye mud . . .

"This day we forded three large rivers, the Conestoga ye last, which came into ye carriage, and wet our feet, and frightened more than one of us."

In 1796 an English scientist, Francis Baily made a journey on horseback from Washington to Pittsburgh by way of Chambersburg, Bedford, and Greensburg, and his account gives a good description of conditions at that relatively early time :[2]

"There being no turnpikes in America, the roads are, of course, very bad in winter, though excellent in summer. I waited nearly a week before I could proceed on my journey, the roads being rendered impassable. There is, at present, but one turnpike-road on the continent, which is between Lancaster and Philadelphia, a distance of 62 miles, and is a masterpiece of its kind. It is paved with stone the whole way, and overlaid with gravel, so that it is never obstructed during the most severe season. This practice is going to be adopted in other parts of that public-spirited state (Pennsylvania), though none of the other states have yet come into the measure.

"At about half-past one, October 7th we left Georgetown and started on our journey over the Allegany Mountains to Pittsburgh, travelling on horseback.

"The accommodations we met with on the road were pretty well, considering the short time this country has been settled, and the character and disposition of its inhabitants, which are not those of the most polished nations, but a character and disposition arising from a consciousness of independence, accompanied by a spirit and manner highly characteristic of this consciousness.

"It is not education alone that forms this character of the Americans. It stands upon a firmer basis than this. The means of subsistence being so easy in the country, and their dependence on each other consequently so trifling, that spirit of servility to those above them so prevalent in European manners, is wholly unknown to them; and they pass their lives without regard to the smiles or frowns of men of power . . .

"From our overnight tavern to the Junietta, a branch of the Susquehannah river, is eight miles. The hill terminates at the river, and the road down to it is a narrow winding path, apparently cleft out of the mountain. It so happened that when we came to this defile, a travelling man with a number of pack-horses had just entered it before us, and as it was impossible for us to pass them, we were obliged to follow them down this long winding passage to the river, at their own pace, which, poor animals, was none of the speediest . . .

"The sun, though not set, had been long hid from us by the neighbouring mountains, and would not lend us one ray of light on our melancholy path. We fell into conversation with our fellow-traveller, and found that he had been to Philadelphia, where he had purchased a number of articles necessary to those who live in this part of the country, and which he was going to dispose of in the best manner possible . . .

"The moon had just begun to spread her silver light; and by her assistance we were enabled to reach our destined port. The road, which was carried along the side of a tremendously high hill, seemed to threaten us with instant death, if our horses should make a false step. Embosomed in woods, on a lonely path, we travelled by the kind light of the moon until near eight o'clock, when we reached our place of destination . . .

"Here we found a very comfortable habitation, and a very good accommodation; and though situated at the top of the highest ridge of mountains, we experienced not only the comforts, but also some of the luxuries of life. From the stone which forms the base of this mountain they make mill-stones, which are sent to all parts of the country, and sell from fifteen to twenty and thirty dollars a pair. Land sells on these mountains for two dollars an acre. We found this so comfortable a place, that we stopped here to breakfast the next morning . . .

"On leaving this place we crossed Laurel Hill, which is near nine miles long, and which is the highest ridge of the Apalachian mountains. It is rather a ridge upon a ridge, than a mountain by itself, as it rises upon the Allegany ridge. The perpendicular height of this ridge is 4200 feet; and in crossing it we were not a little incommoded by the cold winds (October) and rain which generally infest the summit.

"This together with the badness of the roads (being nothing but large loose stones), made it one of the most unpleasant rides I ever experienced. It was near dark before we descended this mountain; and we had then to go three miles to a poor miserable hut, where we were obliged to spend the night amidst the whole family and some travellers, all scattered about the same room . . .

"From the foot of the mountains to Pittsburgh is about forty miles, and here we arrived to dinner on the 18th October. The accommodations we met with were, upon the whole, tolerably good; at least, such as a person (considering the country he was travelling in) might bear with: charges rather high. It cost us, together with our horses, two dollars a day each.

"For breakfast we generally used to have coffee, and buckwheat cakes, and some fried venison or broiled chicken, meat being inseparable from an American breakfast; and whatever travellers happened to stop at the same place, sat down at the same table, and partook of the same dishes, whether they were poor, or whether they were rich; no distinction of persons being made in this part of the country . . .

"The wagons which come over the Allegany mountains from the Atlantic states (bringing dry goods and foreign manufactures for the use of the back-country men), return from this place generally empty; though sometimes they are laden with deer and bear skins and beaver furs, which are brought in by the hunters, and sometimes by the Indians, and exchanged at the stores for such articles as they may stand in need of."

One of the few descriptions that we have of the homes which early settlers built along the road was made by the French traveller, F. A. Michaux, who was a well-known Paris botanist and naturalist. He reported on a trip west of the Alleghenies in the year 1802:[3]

"It is not useless to observe here, that in the United States they give often the name of town to a group of seven or eight houses, and that the mode of constructing them is not the same everywhere. At Philadelphia the houses are built with brick. In the other towns and country places that surround them, half, and even frequently the whole, is built with wood; but at places within seventy or eighty miles of the sea, in the central and southern states, and again more particularly in those situated to the westward of the Alleghany Mountains, one third of the inhabitants reside in log houses.

"These dwellings are made with the trunks of trees, from twenty to thirty feet in length, about five inches diameter, placed one upon another, and kept up by notches cut at their extremities. The roof is formed with pieces of similar length to those that compose the body of the house, but not quite so thick, and gradually sloped on each side. Two doors, which often supply the place of windows, are made by sawing away a part of the trunks that form the body of the house. The chimney, always placed at one of the extremities, is likewise made with the trunks of trees of a suitable length; the back of the chimney is made of clay, about six inches thick, which separates the fire from the wooden walls. Notwithstanding this want of precaution, fires very seldom happen in the country places. The space between these trunks of trees is filled up with clay, but so very carelessly, that the light may be seen through in every part; in consequence of which these huts are exceedingly cold in winter, notwithstanding the amazing quantity of wood that is burnt.

"The doors move upon wooden hinges, and the greater part of them have no locks. In the night time they only push them to, or fasten them with a wooden peg. Four or five days are sufficient for two men to finish one of these houses, in which not a nail is used.

"Two great beds receive the whole family. It frequently happens

FIGURE 25. A Conestoga wagon in the private collection
of J. A. Keillor of Wading River, N. Y.

FIGURE 26. A large Conestoga freighter which was owned by several
generations of the Moose family of Perry County, Pa., from the time
it was built in the mid-nineteenth century until the 1950's. The rear
wheels have a diameter of 70 inches.

FIGURE 27. A Conestoga wagon of the farm variety, presently owned by Bruce Myers of Lancaster Co., Pa.

FIGURE 28. The Burgner wagon is a large freighter, with an overall box length of 19 feet, rear wheels of 66 inches diameter, and tires 4 inches wide. *Kittochtining Historical Society of Franklin County, Chambersburg, Pa.*

that in summer the children sleep upon the ground, in a kind of rug. The floor is raised from one to two feet above the surface of the ground, and boarded. They generally make use of feather beds, or feathers alone, and not mattresses. Sheep being scarce, the wool is very dear; at the same time they reserve it to make stockings. The clothes belonging to the family are hung up around the room, or suspended upon a long pole."

"Inns are very numerous in the United States, and especially in the little towns; yet almost everywhere, except in the principal towns, they are very bad, notwithstanding rum, brandy, and whiskey (they give the name of whiskey, in the United States, to a sort of brandy made with rye), are in plenty. In fact, in houses of the above description all kinds of spirits are considered the most material, as they generally meet with great consumption. Travellers wait in common till the family go to meals. At breakfast they make use of very indifferent tea, and coffee still worse, with small slices of ham fried in the stove, to which they sometimes add eggs and a broiled chicken. At dinner they give a piece of salt beef and roasted fowls, and rum and water as a beverage. In the evening, coffee, tea and ham. There are always several beds in the room where you sleep. Seldom do you meet with clean sheets. Fortunate is the traveller who arrives on the day they happen to be changed; although an American would be quite indifferent about it."

On the road west from Philadelphia, in 1805, Robert Sutcliff encountered some newly arrived immigrants who appealed to him so much that he wrote:[4]

"[At the] General Paoli tavern, I met a family who had landed a few days before in Philadelphia, and were now on their way to the Ohio. The men wore a plain jacket and trousers, with very large shallow crowned hats, and the women had their hair plaited in long braids, which hung down their backs, with jackets and petticoats just the reverse of the fashion of the present day.

"Altogether they had the appearance of a stout, hardy race, and in the company, I understand there were four generations. The master of the inn informed me that he had every reason to believe they had a very large property with them in the wagon in which they travelled."

Sister Catherine Fritsch and half a dozen others travelled from Bethlehem to Philadelphia in May, 1810, and crossed the Lancaster Turnpike at Downingtown. She noticed "ten wagons that stood at a wayside mill to be loaded with flour for the city", and made the following observations about toll gates and the abundance of traffic on the road:[5]

"At the toll-gates their keepers were usually busily engaged in taking the toll, for sometimes three or four conveyances stood in waiting. Some of the gatekeepers kept tally of the money they took in on a slate. Coming early to the toll-gate we had to wait until the sleepy Keeper, rubbing his eyes, came out for our toll. Generally these gatekeepers were taciturn, sour-looking men. Indeed, they seemed to me to resemble each other so much that I almost believed them to be one of the family—sons of one father.

"The more one approaches to the city, the greater the number of conveyances of all kinds, and consequently the deeper the dust which covered us from head to foot, and even filled our mouths. We could not see objects twenty feet ahead of us."

Josiah Quincy described the first part of a trip he made from Philadelphia to Washington:[6]

"At three o'clock this morning (February 10, 1826) the light of a candle under the door, and a rousing knock, told me it was time to depart, and shortly after I left Philadelphia by the Lancaster stage, otherwise a vast illimitable wagon, with seats without backs, capable of holding some sixteen passengers with decent comfort themselves, and actually encumbered with some dozen more. After riding till eight o'clock, we reached the Breakfast House, where we partook of a good meal. We then proceeded through a most beautiful tract of country, where good fences and huge stone barns proved the excellence of the farming. The road seemed actually lined with 'Conestoga' wagons, each drawn by six stalwart horses, and ladened with farm produce."

REFERENCES—
1. Faris, John T. (1917) *Old Roads out of Philadelphia:* Lippincott, Philadelphia.
2. Baily, Francis (1796) "A Journal of a Tour in Unsettled Parts of North America." Reprinted in *Historic Highways of America,* by Archer Butler Hulbert (1904), Arthur H. Clark Co., Philadelphia.
3. Michaux, F. A. (1805) *Travels to the Westward of the Allegany Mountains, in the State of Ohio, Kentucky, and Tennessee:* London. Also in Thwaites (1904) *Early Western Travels,* v. III; Cleveland.
4. Sachse, Julius F. (1912) *The Wayside Inns on the Lancaster Roadside between Philadelphia and Lancaster:* J. F. Sachse, Lancaster, Pa.
5. The source of this quotation has been lost.
6. Gossler, Jacob (1888) *An Old Turnpike Road:* The Baker and Taylor Co., New York.

Chapter 6
Taverns Along the Way

I T IS not hard to imagine how eagerly the weary wagoner looked forward to bringing his "inland ship of commerce" into harbor for the night. With fifteen miles of rugged or cold or dusty or hot road behind him, he must have been more than eager to drop anchor at a friendly tavern and take his ease. Once in the wagon yard, with his horses taken care of, he could look forward to a good meal, some drinks and songs with his friends, and an evening of carefree relaxation.

After 1800 the better traveled pikes contained inns in abundance. Each displayed a conspicuous sign, often four by five feet in size, mounted on stout posts at the highway's edge. Having a painted figure as well as the necessary words, the signs were distinguishable even to the most illiterate. The painting of the signs often was done by itinerant artists, and frequently they worked with considerable skill. Tavern owners were intensely proud of their trade marks. In Lancaster County there were such taverns as The Hickory Tree, The Sorrel Horse, The Fish, The Lamb, The Cat, The Swan, The Western, The Red Lion, The Grape, The Plow, The Globe, The Hat, The Green Tree, The Eagle, The Three Crowns, Cross Keys, The Sign of the Buck, The Sign of the Ship, The Hen and Chickens, and many others, distinguished by pictures as well as names.

Sometimes the landlord chose the name of some dignitary for his tavern, and had his sign embellished with a painted bust of his hero. Among these Washington, of course, was chief, but Lafayette, Lee, Gates, Wayne, and other generals of the Revolution as well as Hancock, Adams, Jefferson, Madison, Monroe, and Franklin frequently were met.

Although the taverns along the road were numerous, the dusty, rough wagoner was not necessarily welcome at all of them. Stages carrying passengers of better dress and better manners stopped at stage houses, which offered the best of accommodations and the most costly. These stage houses often were stop-over points for the stages, where horses were exchanged, and where stage passengers took their meals and lodging for the night (FIG. 36, 37). The fame of their hosts spread far and wide, as well as their reputations for good food and drink. These inns were located at intervals of about twelve miles, where possible, but of course as road traffic increased, other inns and taverns were developed at convenient locations.

Wagoners put up at establishments known as wagon stands, which catered almost exclusively to wagoners and drovers. Here there were no bedrooms, as there sometimes were at the stage houses. The men of the road, or pike boys as they became known, spread their bed rolls down on the floor of the common room, and slept side by side. Searight had first hand knowledge about most of the wagon stands along the National Road from Baltimore to Wheeling, and in his book, *The Old Pike,* he mentions many of these inns together with their proprietors, and tells about the life associated with them.[1]

Searight gives this colorful picture of taverns in the mountains: "On the mountain division taverns were especially numerous. Here one could be seen perched high on its elevated site; there another lay half hidden behind a clump of trees. All of them presented cheerful fronts toward the tired visitor with their colorful pictures and golden letters winking in the sun, ogling the wayfarer from the hot roadbed, and offering him every promise of good cheer. Nearby, the big trough, overflowing with fresh clear water, and the ground below sprinkled with fragrant peppermint, lent a charm to the scene that was well nigh enchanting."

The busy life surrounding one of these wagon stands is well shown in a painting of the Fairview Inn, built in 1801 and located about three miles from Baltimore on the road to Wheeling (FIG. 38). This painting, now owned by the Maryland Historical Society in Baltimore, was made in 1827 when this type of travel was in its classical period. Six Conestoga wagons can be seen in the wagon yard of the inn, and a seventh, in the foreground, is turning into the yard. At least five other Conestogas are visible on the crowded road in front of the inn in addition to a stage coach with its prancing horses and a drover with a herd of cattle.

A necessary adjunct to every wagon stand was the wagon yard at the side or rear, where teams and wagons were driven to stay the night. The six-horse teams rarely were stabled, and instead stood in the open under the sky, winter and summer, rain or pleasant weather. Fenced fields, and pens also were provided for accommodation of the numerous drovers on the road.

The host of a well-run stand would provide each newly arrived wagoner with a gear pole, which was a sapling that was stuck between the spokes of the rear wheels to provide a place to hang the harness.[1] After the horses were unhitched and watered, the feed trough was brought out from its place at the back of the wagon, and mounted up front on the tongue where it was available to the team and at a convenient height. The trough was filled with grain purchased from the tavern, or possibly from the wagoner's own supply if he was not a regular. The horses lined up three to a side and ate their fill. If the night was cold, blankets came out and each horse was covered carefully before the wagoner picked up his own bed roll and went inside to look after his own comfort. On warm summer nights many a wagoner preferred to return to his team after eating, to sleep in the open.

These wagoners who guided the lumbering Conestogas through the valleys and over the mountains, in good weather and bad, were toughened by the vigorous life to the point of despising comforts. They feared nothing and were intensely proud of their teams, their wagons, and their work. They indulged excessively in Monongohela, puffed on their stogies, lived to a ripe old age, and generally died within a few miles of where they had spent much of their lives. Many wagoners saved enough money from their wagoning to purchase their own wagon stands beside the road in later life.

A warm welcome was one thing the weary wagoner could look forward to as he pushed his way into the crowded tavern. The keeper of the tavern knew how to entertain his guests agreeably. Almost every old tavern had its odd shaped little bar, ornamented with fancy lattice work. It was well stocked with locally made whiskey at reasonable prices. Sometimes the landlord would place numerous bottles of liquor on the narrow counter of the little bar, so that all could have free access to them.

It has been said that few of the old tavern keepers made much of a profit from the sale of liquor, but sold it more as an accommodation than as a great source of revenue. Many tavern keepers kept a record of the amount of liquor charged to each customer by jotting it down on a slate behind the bar, in full view of all. When a pint of whiskey was purchased on temporary credit, the letter P was written on the slate, and Q would be entered there when a quart was taken. Some of the heavier users, after treating themselves and their friends, would have accumulated a number of P's and Q's under their name, and eventually the proprietor would remind these fellows that their bills were mounting up by cautioning them "Mind your P's and Q's."

The old tavern keepers, as a whole, were a remarkable group of men. Most often they owned their own establishments, and were influential men in their respective neighborhoods. They were honorable in their dealings, and believed that every man's word was as good as his bond. As caterers they made little display. No bills of fare nor fine linen were offered, but when the call came to "fall to" at the big table at the end of the room, the hungriest of guests would find before them a spread of hearty food that guaranteed to leave them happy and satisfied.

At a wagon stand in the early nineteenth century a good meal might cost 12 1/2¢ and a stiff drink 3¢. The total bill for a wagoner and his horses for an overnight stay would be under $1.75. These prices can be converted into mid-twentieth century equivalents by multiplying by about eight, and if this is done they appear comparable with 1960 prices.

Wagoners turned out early, in order to be on their way when daylight came. After a hearty breakfast their first interest was to care for their horses. This included feeding, watering, currying, and then harnessing them for the day. In winter months most of this work was done by the dim light of a candle lantern.

The taverns provided not only rest and lodging for the passing wagoners (FIG. 39). They also were meeting places for members of the community, as inns and taverns have been in various parts of the world for centuries. They were the favorite resorts for citizens who wished at times to escape from the drudge and ennui of their rural homes, to gaze upon the greater world as it passed by on the road and brought itself to the table and fireside of the inn. Here neighbor met neighbor, sipped their whisky and smoked their stogies together and discussed their home affairs, politics, and other questions of the day.

Jacob Gossler, a resident of Columbia, Pa., writing many years ago, gives his recollections of a scene in that town:[2]

"My father kept the inn or tavern on the street fronting the river [Susquehanna], not far from the entrance to the bridge; the road passed directly by the house, and as a boy, I had ample opportunity to notice the daily panorama moving past—east and west, north and south. I recollect the coaches and wagons, carriages and horses, immense herds of cattle from the far west and southwest, on their way to eastern cities, droves of horses, swine and sheep, and even turkeys, some with heads proud and erect, others with tired, drooping wings—all quietly following the leader.

"Projecting from the second story of the inn, on an iron crossbar, swung an image of General George Washington in courtly coat, sombre 'tights' and buckled shoes, and at his side a splendid sword. In spite of the wind and rain and exposed position, he preserved his awful serenity—and condescendingly looked down on the suspended 'Sorrel Horse' which pranced constantly but ineffectually in front of the rival inn, on the opposite side of the street. I thought the sign a remarkable work of genius and have often since wondered why it was not presented to some museum, or to make famous some art gallery!

"The stern dignity of the Father of his Country, and his severe and majestic attitude, have never been effaced from my memory, nor has any other picture I have ever seen so completely realized my conception of Washington. I have seen pictorial representations of General Andrew Jackson, with his stiff, bristling, upright hair, that might possibly had a more terrifying effect on the British, but nothing could so effectually suppress all attempts at familiarity on the part of the soldiers and civilians, friend or foes, as this swinging sign to which I look back with so much reverence."

On Market Street in Philadelphia stood the Conestoga Wagon Inn, which advertised its presence in newspapers in 1750, as already has been mentioned. There can be little doubt that the proprietor of this inn helped to make the words "Conestoga wagon" well known by choosing the name that he did. References to this inn during the Revolutionary War also have been mentioned earlier. The building was located between Fourth and Fifth Streets, on the south side, at number 410. In 1791 it was kept by Mary Nicholls. In the same year there was an inn nearby, at 432 kept by Nathaniel Brown, and another, the Black Bear at 434, was kept by John Stein.[3]

REFERENCES—
1. Searight, T. B. (1894) *The Old Pike, A History of the National Road:* T. B. Searight, Pub., Uniontown, Pa.
2. Gossler, Jacob (1888) *An Old Turnpike Road:* The Baker and Taylor Co., New York.
3. Jackson, Joseph (1926) *America's Most Historic Highway, Market Street, Philadelphia:* John Wanamaker, New York.

Chapter 7
Lore of the Wagoners

WAGONERS, as a group, were rough and ready outdoorsmen who were not inclined to write down in diaries or journals the accounts of their everyday life on the road. The little that we know about their lives and customs, other than what Searight has written has come largely from stories that have been passed down in families from generation to generation. Even old account books of freighters are scarce.

More than a century ago Moses Hartz, a young man of nineteen years, arrived in the Conestoga Valley of Lancaster County in search of work. The following account of Hartz has been related by H. H. Stoltzful, of Elverson, Pennsylvania, great, great nephew of the former guardian of young Hartz. The youth applied for work at the home of Mr. Mast, a farmer, a former teamster, and the forefather of what later proved to be a family of teamsters. Mast turned the stranger away, telling him that he had no such employment as the young man desired.

The penniless youth, with his worldly possessions under his arm, turned away, downhearted. As he walked down the path from the farmhouse the heart of the old farmer was touched, and he called to him to come back. Mast noted that he was well built and strong and seemed to have the promise of developing into a useful farm hand, so he consented to give him work and to take him into his home, for a while, at least. Hartz proved his worth on the farm during the summer and attracted the attention of the neighbors by his honest and trustworthy habits and his willingness to undertake hard work.

In the fall the farmer fitted up young Hartz with a Conestoga wagon, and six horses with bells, and told him to wend his way to Pittsburgh and on to Ohio. He was instructed to take on any hauling he could get en route, and to bring from Ohio a load of clover seed for the use of the Conestoga Valley farmers for their spring planting. He was requested to be certain to get back in plenty of time to help to do the spring farm work. With those parting words young Moses

Hartz started his career as a teamster across the sparsely settled mountains of Pennsylvania.

For some time Hartz and his team were in a sense lost to the world. Means of communication were such that the young man did not correspond with his guardian throughout the severe, but relatively short, winter season, and he was not expected to do so. Days, weeks, and months passed and eventually the warm days of spring made an early appearance. The time had come for him to make his way back to the fertile farm in the Conestoga Valley, but the days of spring went by and Hartz failed to show up. Mr. Mast grew anxious, then alarmed about his failure to return, and eventually the suspense of waiting became so great that the old teamster decided he would go in search of the tardy wagon. From among the horses in his stable he chose a trusty rider, and set out to the westward in hope of learning of the fate of the wagon.

Mast rode on to Pittsburgh and beyond, into Ohio. There he encountered the young man on his way east with the load of clover seed. The team was sleek looking and in excellent shape, and Hartz was in a most happy mood. Mast was about to reprimand his ward for his tardiness when Hartz drew forth a large sum of money which he had earned for his guardian over and above his expenditures. He had been doing short hauls in the Ohio region, and business had been so good that he had been reluctant to terminate the work and return to the east. The old Pennsylvanian was pleased with the report and immediately proceeded back to Lancaster County, leaving the young man with the load of clover seed to find his way back at the slower pace of the wagon.

By the time Moses Hartz got home clover seed had advanced in price, and the Conestoga Valley farmer sold it at a much greater price than he had expected. The young man had proven himself to be a trustworthy and able worker. With this initial trip he inaugurated a long career as a teamster.

As was the custom in those days, Hartz worked on a farm during the summer season and teamed to the west in the winter. He was what was commonly called a Militia teamster. Moses proved to be a good manager, an indefatigable worker, and a righteous man. He attended, and later joined, the church of which the Masts were life-long members, the Old Order Amish Congregation. He married a young woman of the same congregation, and later he became a Bishop in charge of the church.

Moses Hartz's career as a teamster, farmer, and minister was a remarkable one. He often told of how he started farming with "five wheels," the four on his old Pitt wagon and a wheelbarrow. He and his wife were industrious, self-sacrificing individuals who worked six days of the week and walked or rode horseback many miles to attend religious services on the Sabbath. He became one of the most prosperous farmers in Lancaster County, was a much-respected citizen, a leader in his community, and was reputed to be the owner of the largest farm in Conestoga Valley. He was hale, hearty, and robust, and managed to ward off the calls of a physician all his life. He accumulated wealth, and died at ninety eight.

A newspaper account dated May 28, 1830, describes an accident involving a Conestoga wagon as follows:[1] "A Lancaster stage loaded with thirteen passengers was overturned at Fahnstock's Tavern twenty-one miles from Philadelphia. Mr. McClure and his daughter from Carlisle were seriously hurt and others were considerably bruised. The accident happened when a Conestoga wagon loaded with iron kept the middle of the road and the driver of the stage in trying to pass went over the bank. No blame was attributed to the driver of the stage but rather the teamster of the wagon who cared little for the safety of the lighter vehicle."

There were, of course, a variety of men involved in wagoning. Some long-distance wagoners reputedly were so religious that they refused to move their wagons on Sunday. Others cared not at all for such religious practices. But whether religiously inclined or not, they remained loyal to a tradition, and "stuck by their teams," often refusing to take shelter from a rain if the team had to remain unsheltered. Tradition has it that feats of strength by wagoners included lifting a one hundred pound keg of nails onto a wagon by grasping the narrow edge of the keg between the fingers and thumb of one hand, unloading a six hundred pound barrel of molasses single handed, lifting half a ton of pig iron to win a wager, and lifting a wagon box off of the running gear by lying under it and pushing upward with both hands and feet.

A wagoner used to demonstrate his ability to drive by word of mouth by lying flat on his back in the middle of a field. Then merely by talking to his horses, he would guide the six horses and wagon over his body, turn them around, and have them repass over him again without getting off the flat of his back.

During cold weather wagon wheels sometimes were driven onto planks at night time to prevent them from freezing in the mud. Horses which had stood still on muddy ground all night sometimes were frozen fast in the morning.

Wagoners of old frequently wore a long frock similar to, and undoubtedly derived from, the traditional hunting shirt of frontier America. Searight wrote about it as follows:[2] "Many old wagoners wore a curious garment called a hunting shirt. It was of woolen stuff, after the style of 'blue jeans', with a large cape trimmed in red. It was called a hunting shirt because [it was] first used by hunters in the mountains."

By the time of the American Civil War Conestoga wagoning already was regarded as a romantic occupation of the past. In keeping with the romantic spirit of the middle and late nineteenth century, a few poets took time to remember the wagoner, and to pass on something about his life and world. In 1863 a poem entitled "The Wild Wagoner" by Thomas Buchanan Read was published.[3] This gives a colorful picture of the inland ships of commerce and of the "feared and famous wagoner."

THE WILD WAGONER OF THE ALLEGHENIES

by *Thomas Buchanan Read*

In days long gone, "The Ship and Sheaf"
Was deemed of goodly inns the chief:—
"The Ship," — because its ample door
Fronted the barks that lined the shores,
    Where oft the sun, o'er Delaware,
Looking 'twixt masts and cordage bare,
Their shadows threw on the sanded floor,
    Sailing a phantom vessel there.

And there the crews from far-off climes
Reeled in and sang their rough sea-rhymes,
With a laughter learned from the ocean gale,
As clinked their dripping cupt of ale;
While froth was dashed o'er many a lip,
Like foam against a speeding ship,
And tables chronicled in scars
The tankards and the thirsty tars.

"The Sheaf," — because the wagoner there,
  The captain of the highway ship,
Fresh breathing of his mountain air,
  Hung on the wall his coat and whip;
And farmer, bringing his store to town,
And drover, who drove his cattle down,
  Conversed of pastures and of sheaves,
The season's drouth, or ruinous rain,
Or told of fabulous crops of grain,
  Or fields where grazed incredible beeves.

Twas April, and the evening winds
Were rattling at the open blinds;
The sign, upon its hinge of rust,
Made dreary answer to the gust,
That smote the masts like an ocean squall,
And, whistling, mocked the boatswain's call.

The latch went up; the door was thrown
Aside, as by a tempest blown;
While, bold as an embodied storm,
Strode in a dark and stalwart form,
And all the lights in the sudden wind
Flared as he slammed the door behind.

The noisy revellers ceased their din,
    And into the corner skulked the cur
As the startled keeper welcomed in
    The feared and famous wagoner!
Not long they brooked the keen eye-glance
Who gazed into that countenance;
And even in his mildest mood
His voice was sudden, loud, and rude
As is a swollen mountain stream.
He spoke as to a restive team.
His team was of the wildest breed
    That ever tested wagoner's skill:
Each was a fierce unbroken steed,
    Curbed only by his giant will;
And every hostler quaked with fear
What time his loud bells wrangled near.

On many a dangerous mountain-track,
While oft the tempest burst its wrack,
When lightning, like his mad whip-lash,
Whirled round the team its crooked flash,
    And horses reared in firey fright,
While near them burst the thunder-crash,
    Then heard the gale his voice of might.
The peasant from his window gazed,
    And staring through the darkened air,
Saw, when the sudden lightning blazed,
    The fearful vision plunging there!

And oft on many a wintry hill
    He dashed from out the vale below,
    And heaved his way through drifts of snow,
While all his wheels, with voices shrill,
    Shrieked to the frosty air afar,
    As if December's tempest-car
Obeyed the winter's maniac will.

Ye knew him well, ye mountain-miles
Throughout your numerous dark defiles: —
Where Juniata leaps away
On feathery wings of foam and spray;
Or queenly Susquehanna smiles,
Proud in the grace of her thousand isles;
Where Poet and Historian fling
Their light o'er classic Wyoming;

And you, ye green Lancastrian fields,
Rich with the wealth which Ceres yields;
And Chester's storied vales and hills,
   In depth of rural calm divine,
   Where reels the flashing Brandywine,
And dallies with its hundred mills.

A poem rich with information about wagoning and the wagoner's life, simply entitled "Wagoning", was written and published in 1888 by H. L. Fisher of York, Pennsylvania.[4] Fisher lived in mid-nineteenth century Pennsylvania, and undertook to preserve something of the life of olden times which he saw passing away round about him. This poem is from the book *Olden Times: or Pennsylvania Rural Life, Some Fifty Years Ago, and Other Poems.*

WAGONING

by *H. L. Fisher*

There were two classes of these men, —
   Men of renown, not well agreed;
"Militia-men" drove narrow treads,
Four horses and plain red Dutch beds,
   And always carried "grub" and feed;
Because they carried feed and "grub"
They bore the brunt of many a "rub."

These were the thrifty farmers' teams
  That wagoned, only, now and then;
They made their trips in winter-time
They trudged along through rime and grime
  And hurried through it, back again;
An annual trip, or two, they made,
And drove a sort of coastwise trade.

They gathered up promiscuous loads
  Of produce in the neighborhood—
Some whiskey, flour and cloverseeds,
To suit a city dweller's needs,
  And always did the best they could,
By hauling these to Baltimore—
Back-loaded for some country-store.

The "Reg'lars" boldly ventured out,
  Despising danger, doubt, and fear;
And, like the gallant merchant-ships,
They made their long, continuous trips
  All through the seasons of the year:
No matter whether cold or warm—
Through heat and cold, through calm and storm.

I've seen a many a fleet of them
  In one, long, upward, winding row;
It ever was a pleasant sight,
As seen from distant mountain-height,
  Or quiet valley, far below;
Their snow-white covers looked like sail,
From mountain-height or distant vale.

I see them on their winding way,
  As, in the merry olden time
I saw them, with their heavy loads,
Upon the old-time turnpike-roads,
  The rugged mountains climb;
Like full-rigged ships they seemed to glide
Along the deep-blue mountain-side.

The "Regulars" were haughty men,
    Since *five* or *six* they always drove,
With broad-tread wheels and English beds,
They bore their proud and lofty heads,
    And always thought themselves above
The homespun, plain, Militia-men,
Who wagoned only now and then.

(Who has not seen, who has not felt
    The cursed arrogance of *purse!*
E'en in the wagoners of the past,
Was seen the haughtiness of caste,
    And felt, the old, old, social curse,
That measures manhood by success
More than by native nobleness.)

So were all goods transported then—
    By reg'lar or militia team—
And, though, a slow and toilsome way,
It was the best known in its day—
    Before the world had got up steam—
As, now, this steam-dependent world
Is round its business-axle whirled.

I hear the music of the wheels,
    Slow moving o'er the frozen snow;
Like distant bugle-notes they sound,
While from the mountain-heights, around,
    Or from the dark-green depths below,
Perchance, the music of the bells
The weird, enchanting, echo swells.

I hear the wagoner's hoarse, harsh voice
    Still urging on the lab'ring steeds;
I hear the sharp crack of his whip—
I see the horses pull and slip,
    Still urged to move herculean deeds—
The while their steaming breath congeals
Like hoar-frost, on the wintry fields.

FIGURE 29. A Conestoga wagon of the farm type, but having an unusually great up-sweep at the front end. This now is part of the wagon collection at the Pennsylvania Farm Museum of Landis Valley. *Penna. Turnpike Commission.*

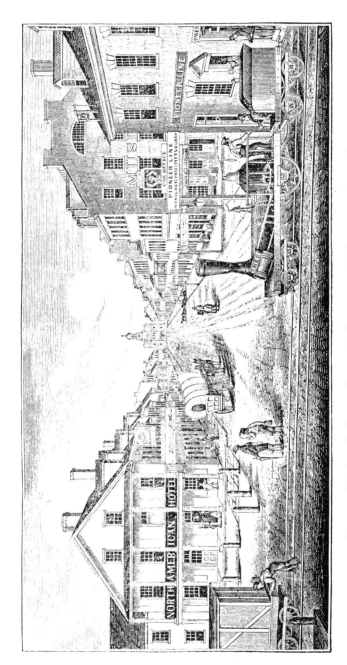

FIGURE 30. North Queen Street, in Lancaster, 1843, as seen from the north. In the foreground is the Pioneer Line Railroad, and in the center a Conestoga wagon. *Historical Collections of the State of Pennsylvania by Sherman Day, Philadelphia 1843.*

O'er mountain-heights and valleys deep,
   Still, slowly on and on they move,
Along their tedious, rugged, way—
Some eighty furlongs in a day—
   Their stalwart strength and faith they prove,
And oft' to their extreme delight,
Some old-time tavern looms to sight.

There, Custom always called a halt,
   To water, rest, and take a drink;
And, not unlikely, while they stopped,
A jig was danced, or horses swapped;
   And so, perchance, a broken link,
The smith was hurried to renew,
Or tighten up a loosened shoe.

Meantime, the jolly wagoners stood
   And swaggered 'round the old-time bar—
The latticed nook, the landlord's throne,
Where he presided, all alone,
   And smoked his cheap cigar,
And reckoned up the tippler's bill
For whiskey, at a "fip" a gill;

Or other kinds of old-time drinks,
   All full of good and hearty cheer;
As apple-jacks, and peach-brandies
Or cider-oils, or sangarees,
   Or, O, the foaming poker'd-beer;
Or apple-toddies, steaming hot,
Or cherry-bounce—almost forgot.

There never was a rougher set,
   Or class of men upon the earth,
Than wagoners on the Reg'lar line—
Nor jollier when in their wine,
   Around a blazing bar-room hearth;
How did they fiddle dance and sing?
How did the old-time bar-room ring?

There were few idle fiddles when
   Old wag'ners drank their jolly fill
Of beer and cider by the quart
And wines and gins of every sort,
   And whiskey, measured by the gill,
And cherry-bounce and cider oil,
And bitters spiced with penny-royal

Sometimes the question—who should treat
   Was left to doubtful luck, or chance;
A game of cards at whist, or loo,
Of checkers, chess, or domino;
   And after that the hoe-down dance;
Sometimes the question—who had beat?
Was settled by the landlord's treat.

Around a blazing hearth, at e'en,
   Or roaring ten-plate Pinegrove stove,
Those heroes of the turnpike-roads—
Those haulers of the heavy loads,
   Or weary drivers of a drove,
Forgathered, many a winter's night
In freedom, fun, and fond delight.

They sat in all the different ways
   That men could sit, or ever sat;
They told of all their jolly days,
And spat in all the different ways
   That men could spit, or ever spat;
They talked of horses and their strength,
And spun their yarns at endless length.

Sometimes they raffed for the stakes,
   And sometimes shot therefor at mark;
A many a foolish wager laid,
And many a reckless swap was made—
   Of horses—traded in the dark;
Sometimes disputes ran wild and high,
To bloody nose or blacken'd eye.

All such disputes were ended quick
     By an appeal to harden'd fists;
These were the courts of last resort,
That settled pleas of every sort
     That came upon the wagoners' lists;
No other forum, then, was sought,
When *the* decisive fight was fought.

Ten wagoners in a bar-room —well
     Say, twenty feet by scant sixteen;
A ten-plate stove, that weighed a ton,
Stood in a wooden-box-spitoon—
     Which was, of course, not very clean—
'Mid clouds of cheap tobacco-smoke,
Thick, dark, and strong enough to choke.

Huge benches and some pond'rous chairs—
     Such as the world no more may see;
An ample pile of hickory logs,
An old tom-cat and several dogs,
     And playful pups—some two or three—
All 'round one stove or bar-room fire!
A scene an artist might admire.

And, superadded to all these
     Were unwashed feet and shoes and boots,
And boot-jacks, slippers, tallow-dips,
And some great-coats and Louden whips
     And heaps of wagoners' oversuits;
While currying-shirts and overalls
Embellished the surrounding walls.

But O, the kitchen of an inn—
     That heaven on earth in days of yore!
The pots and pans and ovens—dutch,
The home-baked bread we loved so much—
     The want of which we now deplore,
While vainly seeking nutriment
In alka*lies* for ailment.

There, buxom lasses and their beaus,
　　On winter-nights, in olden times,
In freedom sang their merry songs,
And on the shovel, with the tongs,
　　Rang out the rude and rustic chimes;
While on the pond'rous iron crane
Hung pot-rack, hook, and dusty chain:

There, in their homespun woolen gowns,
　　When daily labors were well o'er,
The lasses used to sing and sew,
Or trip the light fantastic toe
　　Upon the burnished kitchen-floor;
And, though around a kitchen-hearth,
The most enchanting place on earth.

How many a troth was plighted there—
　　How many a happy match was made?
How many a legend there was said
By tongues and lips long cold and dead!
　　How many a rougish trick was played
Upon some happy bride and groom
By hands long mouldering in the tomb?

Where are those kitchens of the past—
　　Those rugged chimneys built of stone?
Where is the pitchy fagot's blaze,
Which, like the Borealis-rays,
　　From out the chimney-corner shone?
Like those who danced and frolicked there,
They're numbered with the things that were.

The fragrance of their memory hangs
　　And lingers 'round us like the air;
They haunt us in our waking dreams,
And, often, in our sleep, it seems
　　As if again, we saw them, there;
But stern realities arise
While moisture gathers in our eyes.

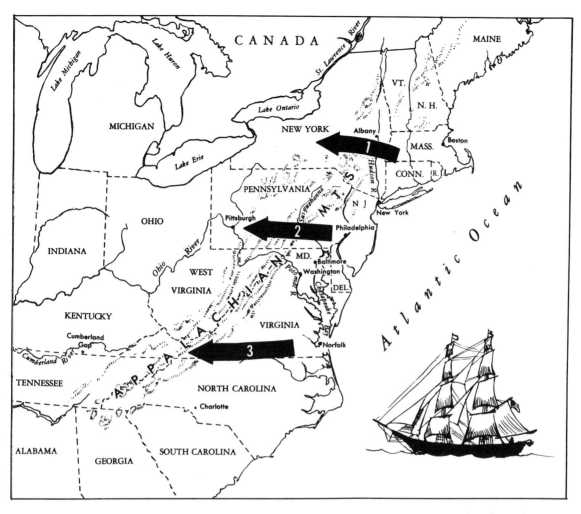

FIGURE 31. The physical barrier of the Appalachian Mountains, and the hostility of the Indians who lived behind them, severely restricted the flow of settlers into the Ohio Valley until after the American Revolution. There were three possible routes across or around the mountains, indicated by the large arrows. The northern route, through the Mohawk Valley (#1), was out of the way for most of the potential emigrants, and did not lead to the right place anyway. The southern route (#3) was long and difficult. The central route (#2) through southern Pennsylvania and the Potomac Valley became the funnel through which most of the people poured.

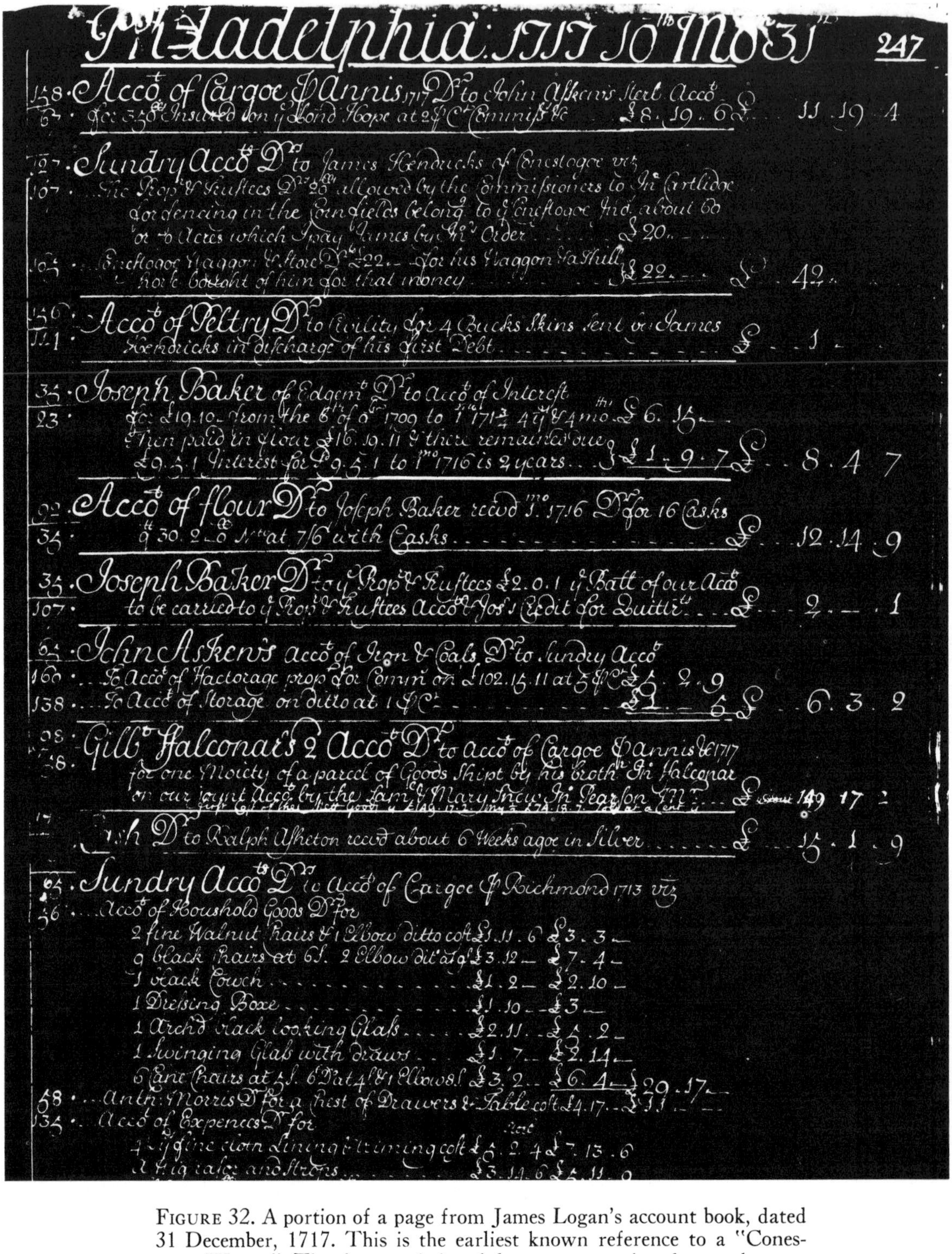

Philadelphia: 1717 10th mo 31 247

Acco of Cargoe Annis 1717 Dr to John Askew's Sterl. Acco for 350 Insured on y Bond Hope at 2½ P Ct Comissi &c £8. 19. 6 £ 11. 19. 4

Sundry Accots Drs to James Hendricks of Conestogoe viz
The Props & Trustees Drs 20 allowed by the Commissioners to Jn Cartlidge for fencing in the Cornfields belonging to y Conestogoe Ind about 60 or 70 Acres which I pay James by his Order £20.
Conestogoe Waggon & Store Dr £22. For his Waggon & a Thill horse bought of him for that money £22. £ 42.

Acco of Peltry Dr to Civility for 4 Bucks Skins sent by James Hendricks in discharge of his first Debt £ 1.

Joseph Baker of Edgemt Dr to Acco of Interest for £19.10. from the 6th of 6 mo 1709 to 1st 1713 4 y & 4 mo £ 6. 15.
Then paid in flour £16. 19. 11 & there remained due £9. 5. 1 Interest for £9. 5. 1 to 1st mo 1716 is 2 years £1. 9. 7 £ 8. 4. 7

Acco of flour Dr to Joseph Baker recd 1 mo 1716 Dr for 16 Casks q 30. 2. 0 at 7/6 with Casks £ 12. 14. 9

Joseph Baker Dr to y Props & Trustees £2. 0. 1 y Ball of our Acco to be carried to y Props & Trustees Acco & Jos's Credit for Quitrents £ 2. . 1

John Askew's Acco of Iron & Coals Dr to Sundry Accots
To Acco of Factorage prop for Comm on £102. 15. 11 at 5 P Ct £5. 2. 9
To Acco of Storage on ditto at 1 P Ct £1. £ 6. 3. 2

Gillt Falconar's 2 Acco Dr to Acco of Cargoe Annis &c 1717 for one Moiety of a parcel of Goods Shipt by his broth Jn Falconar on our joynt Acco by the Sam & Mary Snow Jn Pearson £ 149 17

Cash Dr to Ralph Asheton recd about 6 Weeks agoe in Silver £ 15. 1. 9

Sundry Accots Dr to Acco of Cargoe Richmond 1713 viz
Acco of Houshold Goods Dr for
2 fine Walnut Chairs & 1 Elbow ditto cost £1. 11. 6 £3. 3.
9 black Chairs at 6s. 2 Elbow ditto at 9s £3. 12. £7. 4.
1 black Couch £1. 2. £2. 10.
1 Dressing Boxe £1. 10. £3.
1 Arch'd black Looking Glass £2. 11. £5. 2.
1 Swinging Glass with drawrs £1. 7. £2. 14.
6 Cane Chairs at 5s. 6d at 4 & 1 Elbow 8s £3. 2. £6. 4. £29. 17.
Anth Morris Dr for a Chest of Drawers & Table cost £4. 17.
Acco of Expences Dr for

FIGURE 32. A portion of a page from James Logan's account book, dated 31 December, 1717. This is the earliest known reference to a "Conestogoe Wagon". The characteristics of the wagon mentioned are unknown, of course, but the fact that a "Thill horse" was sold with the wagon suggests that the wagon may have had shafts.

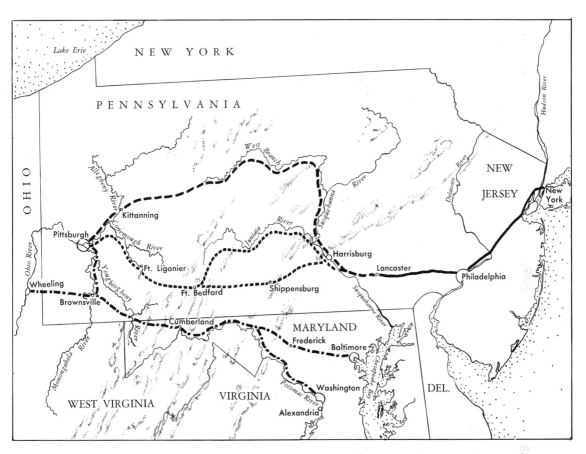

FIGURE 33. The chief wagon routes to Pittsburgh, Wheeling, and the Ohio Valley. The southern route, through Cumberland and Brownsville to Wheeling, was the National Road. Pennsylvania traffic going west from Harrisburg had three choices of route, but the southern roads, through Ft. Bedford and Ft. Ligonier carried most of the traffic.

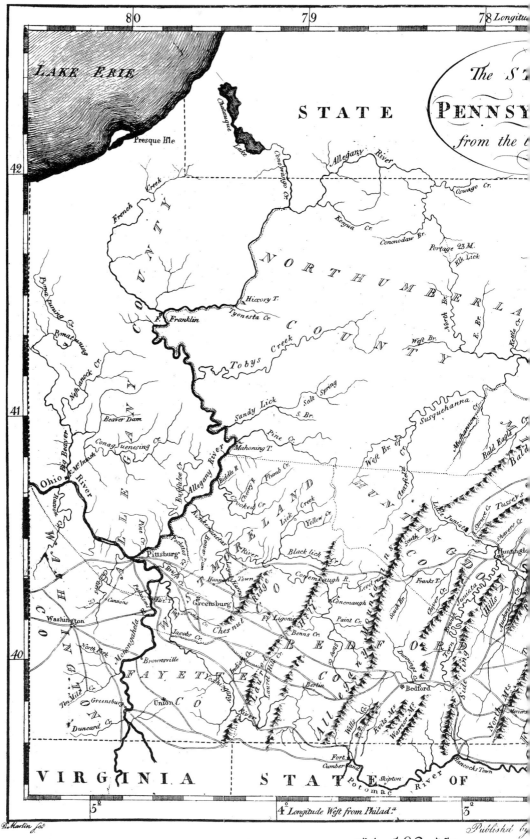

FIGURE 34. This map of Pennsylvania, published in
1794, shows the principal roads which, presumably,
were open to wagon travel at that time.

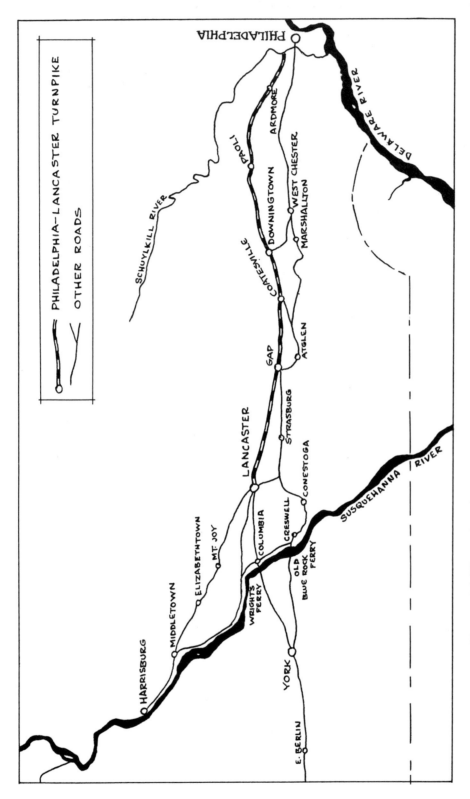

FIGURE 35. The early Conestoga road ran from Philadelphia to the Susquehanna River through the towns of Strasburg and Conestoga. It was begun in 1683 and completed about 1734. The turnpike from Philadelphia to Lancaster was completed in 1794 and was heavily traveled by Conestoga wagons and stage coaches. Traffic from Lancaster to Pittsburgh generally did not cross the river at Columbia, but went to the north to cross at Middletown or Harrisburg.

FIGURE 36. The Valley Inn, built in 1758 and enlarged in 1814, stood about two miles east of York, Pa., on the road to Lancaster. For over two centuries this once-handsome building was a haven for travelers along this well-traveled highway. The building was demolished in November, 1962 for commercial reasons that could not possibly justify the loss of it to the community. Happily, however, stone, timbers, and other salvageable materials from the oldest part of the structure were used for a re-creation of the original smaller building on the grounds of Susquehanna Memorial Gardens, a few miles south of York.

FIGURE 37. The Eagle was an inn that catered to stage coach travelers, apparently. The stage horses are unhitched, for changing, or watering, and the passengers have left the coach. A somewhat fanciful version of a Conestoga wagon is passing by on the road. *From the Collections of the Library of Congress.*

Fisher's poem mentions the wagoners, gay with spirits, singing and dancing in the bar rooms of the taverns. A large portion of the old Pennsylvania population was intensely religious, and heavily frowned upon gaiety, singing, dancing, and drinking. But freedom reigned on the open road, especially for the regular teamsters whose spirits were not so likely to be held in check by the teachings and customs of the religious groups to which they did not belong. The regulars dared to flout the sobering atmosphere whenever it began to settle about them. Their songs, often unfit to print, were at times meaningless, ridiculous, profane, and vulgar. Other songs of the wagoners were the more or less well known songs of early America, such as: Arkansaw Traveller; Barbara Allen; Captain Jinks of the Horse Marines; Chimney Sweep Song; Darby Ram; Die Woch; Doktor Eisenbart; Gickerigie; Joe Bowers; Jordan Am a Hard Road to Trabbel; Lauterbach; Liewer Heindrich; Little Brown Jug; Little More Cider, Too; O Du Lieber Augustin; Old Dan Tucker; Old Joe Clark; O'Reilly; Reuben and Rachael; Schnitzelbank; Sweet Rosy O'Grady; The Girl I Left Behind Me; The Three Crows; There Is a Tavern in the Town; Turkey in the Straw.

The coming of the railroads was viewed as a calamity by the wagoners, and it did, in fact, bring about an end to their way of life. Their feelings about the railroad are well expressed in a song entitled "Wagoners' Curse on Railroad".[5]

WAGONERS' CURSE ON RAILROAD

Come all ye bold wag'ners turn out man by man,
That's opposed to the railroad or any such plan;
'Tis once I made money by driving my team,
But the goods are now hauled on the railroad by steam.

May the devil get the fellow that invented the plan.
It'll ruin us poor wag'ners and every other man.
It spoils our plantations wherever it may cross,
And it ruins our markets, so we can't sell a hoss.

If we go to Philadelphia, inquiring for a load,
They'll tell us quite directly its gone out on the railroad
The rich folks, the plan they may justly admire
But it ruins us poor wag'ners and it makes our taxes higher.

Our states they are indebted to keep them in repair,
Which causes us poor wag'ners to curse and swear.
It ruins our landlords, it makes business worse,
And to every other nation it has only been a curse.

It ruins wheelwrights, blacksmiths, and every other trade.
So Damned be all the railroads that ever was made!
It ruins our mechanics, what think you of it, then?
And it fills our country full of just a lot of great rich men.

The ships they will be coming with Irishmen by loads,
All with their picks and shovels, to work on the railroads,
When they got on the railroad, it is then that they are fixed.
They'll fight just like the devil with their cudgels and their sticks.

The American with safety, can scarcely ever pass,
For they will blacken both his eyes for one word of his sass.
If it wasn't for the torment, I as leave would be in Hell,
As upon the cursed railroad, or upon the canal.

Come all ye bold wag'ners that have got good wives;
Go home to your farms and there spend your lives.
When your corn is all cribbed up and your small grain is sowed.
You'll have nothing else to do but just to curse the damned railroad.

REFERENCES —
1. The name of the newspaper from which this account was taken has been lost.
2. Searight, T. B. (1894) *The Old Pike, A History of the National Road*: T. B. Searight, Pub., Uniontown, Pa.
3. Read, Thomas Buchanan (1863) *Wagoner of the Alleghanies*: J. B. Lippincott and Co., Philadelphia.
4. Fisher, H. L. (1888) *Olden Times: or Pennsylvania Rural Life, Some Fifty Years Ago, and Other Poems*: Fisher Brothers, York, Pa.
5. Korson, Geo., ed. (1949) *Pennsylvania Songs and Ledgends*: University of Pennsylvania Press, Philadelphia. This song was "collected" by Howard C. Frey in the 1920's, and first published with music in this book. One verse of it was published by Searight in 1894. The words also were sung to the tune "Green on the Cape."

Chapter 8
Men Who Made the Wagons

THERE once was a carpenter of York, Pennsylvania, who was so interested in the people about him and what they did, that he devoted much of his free time to making ink and water color sketches of them at their work and play. With a carpenter's inclination for detail, he set down beside these sketches numerous important facts relating to them, and almost always he mentioned the names of the people involved. This took place mainly in the second quarter of the nineteenth century, before the era of the camera. Because of his efforts there exists today an account of life in early York so rich in detail that scarcely any American city has anything to equal it. This man was Lewis Miller.

Wagons, apparently, were such common vehicles that Miller paid little special attention to them. In some of his street scenes, blue Conestogas with their white cloth covers are to be seen along with other wagons and carts. But fortunately, he did pay special attention to the Conestoga wagon in one small sketch (Fig. 40). Here he showed a blue wagon with white cover, and near it made the following remarks: "The wagons made in York had a praise, for the good work done to them at our place, in the woodwork, and the iron work, done — by the — blacksmith shops, the names of masters and shops making wagons, old Frederick Laumaster, & son Jacob, Philip Rupp, Christian Rupp, Christian Lanius, old Jacob Rudy, Daniel Weaver, Joseph Ubdegraff, Jeremiah Hess, James Morris."

"Names of the Black Smith Shops

Adam Graver	Jesse Hines	Peter Rudy
Peter Reisinger	George Stribig	George Shetter
Mathias Gibens	John Small	Michael Weitm.
Jacob Pfleiger	Joseph Hollan	Michael Grabill
Lorence Jacobs	Samuel Hays	Rinart Bott
Samuel Slenfritz	William Rease	John Reisinger
		Mr. Fahs."

Nothing could be more specific. The names of the masters and shops making wagons are given beside a picture of the type of wagon made, and it is stated that the iron work was done by the blacksmith shops.

In an earlier chapter it was pointed out that the center of Conestoga wagon making was southeastern Pennsylvania, and that this also was the region where the famous Pennsylvania longrifle was developed and produced. At the present time we know considerably more about the gunsmithing trade than we do about wagon making. This is because longrifles have been studied to a greater extent than wagons, as a consequence of the considerable interest in them that has been shown by collectors. The fact that longrifles often are signed, either directly with the maker's name, or indirectly through the art work found upon them, has sent interested students searching through early census reports, property tax lists, deeds, wills, church records, graveyards, and other places for precious bits of information about the makers. The quest still is in progress, but the general picture of the gunsmithing trade in early Pennsylvania has begun to unfold.[1,2,3] It seems probable that certain aspects of the wagon making trade will be found to parallel those of gunsmithing, and in studying the Conestoga wagon, this probably is a useful concept to bear in mind. Furthermore, it may be established eventually that some men worked at both trades.

In Europe the gunsmithing trade was tightly controlled by guilds for centuries. A youth who wished to learn the trade was bound to a master for an extensive apprenticeship period. At the end of this period, which often lasted seven years, or even more, the youth became a journeyman, traveling about the country and working in various locations. Later, if his abilities measured up to it, he produced a masterpiece, and the highly honored title of master was conferred upon him by the guild.

The early tradesmen of Pennsylvania worked in the shadow of this rigidly controlled European guild system, which they, or their fathers, or their grandfathers had known in Germany, England, or elsewhere. Probably because of the continually changing nature of the American frontier, the formal guilds did not develop here, but some features of the system were so practical and basic that they inevitably became a part of the American way of doing things. Throughout the eighteenth century, and the first half of the nineteenth century, an American youth wishing to learn a trade often was formally bound to a master by an indenture agreement, in much the same manner as was done in Europe. Relatively few American indenture agreements have been brought to light, however. Kindig[2]

FIGURE 38. The Fairview Inn, built in 1801, was a wagoner's tavern located on the National Turnpike about three miles from Baltimore. This painting was made in 1827, when wagoning along this famous old road was in its classical period. Six Conestogas can be seen in the yard, and a seventh, on the road, is heading toward it. On the busy road in front of the inn there is a stage with its prancing horses, a drover with a herd of cattle, and five other Conestogas. *Maryland Historical Society, Baltimore, Md.*

FIGURE 39. The inn on the road was a center of life. This nineteenth century lithograph by a Baltimore firm shows a variety of activities underway, and in the center, a Conestoga-type farm wagon is stopped for watering of the horses. *From the Collections of the Library of Congress.*

and Kauffman[3] discuss the training of gunsmith apprentices in early Pennsylvania on the basis of the meager information that has been found, and Kauffman presents the wording for the only known gunsmith apprentice indenture.

Undoubtedly the apprentice system also was utilized in the wagon making trade, although the writers do not know of a specific reference which establishes this as a fact. Kauffman[3] reports that indenture records in the office of the mayor of Philadelphia for the early 1770's show apprenticeship periods of 13 years for goldsmiths, 3 years for coopers, 2 years for leather breeches makers, and only 20 months for blacksmiths. Probably it is significant that carpenter Lewis Miller used the word *masters* before giving his list of wagon makers.

The indenture that bound a fledgling wagon maker to his master probably had a close resemblance to an indenture in the allied trade of blacksmithing. William Hatfield, of Fayette County in western Pennsylvania, worked much of his life as a blacksmith along the National Road. His indenture, signed in 1816, is as follows:[4]

This Indenture Witnesseth: That William Hatfield, of the township of Union, in the county of Fayette, State of Pennsylvania, hath put himself by the approbation of his guardian, JOHN WITHROW, and by these presents doth voluntarily put himself an apprentice to GEORGE WINTERMUTE, of the township of Redstone, county and State aforesaid, blacksmith, to learn his art, trade or mystery he now occupieth of followeth, and after the manner of an apprentice to serve him from the day of the date hereof, for and during the full end and term of five years next ensuing, during all which time he, the said apprentice, his master shall faithfully serve, his secrets keep, his lawful commands every where gladly obey; he shall do no damage to his said master, nor suffer it to be done without giving notice to his said master; he shall not waste his master's goods, nor lend them unlawfully to others; he shall not absent himself day or night from his master's service without his leave; he shall not commit any unlawful deed, whereby his said master shall sustain damage, nor contract matrimony within the said term; he shall not buy nor sell, nor make any contract whatsomever, whereby his master receive damage, but in all things behave himself as a faithful apprentice ought to do during the said term. And the said George Wintermute shall use the utmost of his endeavors to teach, or cause to be taught and instructed, the said apprentice the trade or mystery he now occupieth or followeth, and procure and provide for him, the said apprentice, sufficient meat, drink, common working apparel, washing, and lodging, fitting for an apprentice during the said term; and further, he the said master, doth agree to give unto the said apprentice, ten month's schooling within the said term, and also the said master doth agree to give unto the said apprentice two weeks in harvest in each and every year that he, the said apprentice, shall stay with his said master; also the said George Wintermute, doth agree to give unto the said apprentice one good freedom suit of clothes. And for the true performance of all and every the said covenants and agreements, either of the said parties binds themselves to each other by these presents.

In witness thereof, they have interchangeably put their hands and seals, this first day of April, one thousand eight hundred and sixteen.

GEORGE WINTERMUTE
WILLIAM HATFIELD
JOHN WITHROW

Witness present
BENJAMIN ROBERTS

It is unfortunate that Conestoga wagons usually were not signed by their makers. On the front hound iron of existing wagons some initials and dates have been found, but only rarely. A complete name is present on the hound iron of one wagon, but this is an unusual case. For the most part we must admit to the missing link of identification between surviving wagons and the makers whose names can be found in the old records. Because of this there is little reason to compile an extensive list of wagon makers. However, inasmuch as there is so very little known about the early wagon making industry, a list of wagon makers would have value not only for the statistical information it would provide, but also as a starting place for further researches. With these thoughts in mind, a list of wagon makers is given at the end of this chapter. This list was compiled chiefly from tax records of Newbury Township, Hanover Borough, Heidelberg Township, and York Borough, all in York County, Pennsylvania, in the period from 1800 to 1850. It does not represent all of York County.

The town of Hanover lies about fifteen miles southwest of York on the long-used wagon road to Frederick, Maryland. Throughout the early part of the nineteenth century it had a population of less than a thousand. The people there were active craftsmen, and wagon making developed into one of the important trades of the town. Prowell[5] mentions that the town was incorporated in 1815, and at that time the wagon makers were George Eiler, Nicholas Field, George Frysinger, George Grove, John Leaver, and Charles Zeigler. He comments in particular about George Frysinger, who "was a wagon maker and resided on Baltimore Street, where he carried on his business. He made a large number of wagons and disposed of them to the farmers, his trade extending as far south as the Shenandoah Valley of Virginia. Frysinger was an ardent Democrat and served as burgess in the year 1820. During the War of 1812 he commanded a local military company." He again served as burgess in 1834.

Prowell comments further about wagon making at Hanover: "The wagon maker was the pioneer of an industry which became very prominent in this borough for a period of fifty years. From 1830 to 1880 Hanover was known as the leading town in southern Pennsylvania for the manufacture of buggies and other pleasure carriages. During this period there were more than thirty large and small factories, each employing from five to twenty men. Hanover carriages had a wide reputation, and were sold in large numbers in Pennsylvania, Maryland, and Virginia. When this industry was conducted most prosperously, it is estimated that 2,000 carriages or more were made each year at all the different factories in Hanover. Jacob Grove and his brother John succeeded their father in the wagon making business and early began to make buggies."

George Shetter of York Borough was a wagon maker who manufactured cannon carriages and tumbrels during the War of 1812. The York Historical Society has a drawing by Lewis Miller showing Shetter's large shop in operation on this war work, and it can be estimated that fifteen or twenty men were employed there. In the 1840's George Shetter and his son, George Jr., are variously listed in the tax records for York Borough, North Ward, as auger makers, and smiths.

Gunsmithing was a trade that sometimes, if not often, was carried on in a family for a number of generations. Friendships, and at times, marriages between these gunsmithing families were common. The case of "old Frederick Laumaster, & son Jacob," wagon makers suggests that such relationships may have existed among wagon makers too, but probably to a lesser degree. A few longrifles with considerable artistic merit and having York County characteristics are known that bear the signature "J. Lowmaster," but no records have been found that list J. Lowmaster as a gunsmith.[2] It is possible that these rifles were made by Frederick's son, Jacob, even though he was a wagon maker by trade, hence it is desirable to set down as much information about these two men as can be found in the public records and elsewhere.

Frederick Laumaster (also spelled Lowmaster in the same document) paid 49 £ for lot #12 on the south side of High Street (now Market St.), measuring 65 feet by 235 feet. The deed for this transaction is dated 29 August, 1783, and the purchase was from Andrew Anich, barber, and his wife. Lowmaster is mentioned as a wagon maker in the deed. The 1790 census lists Frederick Lowmaster as the head of a household containing three males under the age of sixteen, and three females. On 8 January, 1799 Frederick Lowmaster, wagonmaker, and his wife Mary Magdalena sold the High Street lot #12 for 115 £ to Charles McGovern. Frederick Lowmaster signed his name, his wife used an X for a mark, and the transaction was witnessed by Jacob Updegraff who probably was related to the wagon maker Joseph Updegraff. Frederick's will was recorded 6 February, 1801, and this named his wife, Mary Magdalena, together with wagon makers Christian Lanius and Henry Reissinger as administrators. The 1810 census lists both Jacob and Mary Lowmaster. In 1814 Jacob bought two tracts of land totaling 114 acres in Manheim Township from Magdalene Shirer for 40 £. John Shiery and wife Christina granted a power of attorney to their "beloved friend" Jacob on 22 May 1816, this was witnessed by John Lowmaster of Berkley Co., Virginia. On 3 April 1817 Jacob bought from Shiery and wife a plantation of 114 acres in Manheim Township, for $3420. On 24 April 1825 a Deed of Assignment was filed whereby Jacob Lowmaster, Michael Ebert, and Charles Waiser became trustees for the sale of property of Yost Kuhl and wife.

The 1830 census lists Jacob Lowmaster as head of a large household. There were two girls below five years of age, two boys and one girl between five and ten, two boys and one girl between ten and fifteen, a male between twenty and thirty years, and Jacob and Mary between the ages of forty and fifty.

In 1838 Jacob Lowmaster made a small fortune in one brief day, apparently because of some inside information. On 22 March a deed was recorded, listing him as a wagon maker. He bought from Jacob and Catherine Spangler for $2,000 a half lot on the south side of High Street east of the old court house then in existence. On the land was a two-story dwelling house, a barn, and a Changler shop (sic), i.e. a hardware store or chandler shop. The lot was 32 feet 6 inches wide by 230 feet deep. The next day Jacob and his wife Mary sold the lot to the County of York for $10,000. On March 22nd Jacob bought lot #44, also on the south side of High Street, and of the same size, for $4,000 from Samuel Meyers and his wife Elizabeth. He also bought lot #57 on High Street, for $4,000, from John Gardner on 22 March. In 1853 Jacob was an administrator in the estate of Benjamin Frey. Jacob's will was recorded in 1856 according to an administration bond dated 5 November, and Charles and William Lowmaster are named as administrators. He apparently died intestate in 1863. By a deed dated 4 April 1863 his heirs sold his lot on the south side of High Street to William Lowmaster for $3350. His heirs are listed as Charles Lowmaster and wife Elizabeth of York, David Lowmaster and wife Mary Jane of York, Catherine Keuher and husband John Lowmaster of York, Charles and Eliza Welsh of York, Jacob Lowmaster and wife Jane, and Henry Lowmaster and wife Mary, all of Burlington, N. J., and Joseph O. and Sarah Purkepile of Crawford Co., Ohio.

SOME WAGON MAKERS
OF YORK COUNTY, PENNSYLVANIA, 1800 - 1850

The following wagon makers, coach makers, and wheelwrights worked in York County between 1800 and 1850. Data were obtained from property tax lists and U. S. census lists where occupations often, but not always, are listed. Tax lists for Hanover Borough, Heidelberg Township, and Newbury Township were examined in detail, but most others were not searched. No tax lists dating before 1800 were examined. Abbreviations: B., Borough; T., Township; cm, coach or carriage maker; wm, wagon maker; wr, wheelwright. Dates indicate listings with occupations mentioned.

Althoff, Joseph	Hanover B.	coach maker	1836, 1838, 1839, 1840
Ashmore, Luther	York B.	coach maker	1843
Beamer, William	Newbury T.	wagon maker	1835, 1836
Beard, Charles	Hanover B.	wagon maker	1831, 1832, 1833, 1834, 1838, 1840

Name	Location	Occupation	Years
Beard, Simon	Hanover B.	coach maker	1839, 1840
Becker, John	Paradise T.	wagon maker	1820 census
Boren, Ligismund	Heidelberg T.	wagon maker	1816
Bream, Jacob	Hanover B.	wagon maker	1824, 1825, 1826 cm
Brookhart, Daniel	Newbury T.	wagon maker	1821 wr, 1823 wm
Bucher, Adam	Hanover B.	wagon maker	1819 wm; 1820 census wm
Carter, Samuel	Newbury T.	wheelwright	1823, 1824
Cox, William	Franklin T.	wagon maker	1820 census
Driver, Christian	Fairview T.	wheelwright	1820 census
Drorbough, Peter	Newbury T.	wagon maker	1836, 1837, 1838, 1839
Eiler, George	Heidelberg T.	wagon maker	1816
	Hanover B.	wagon maker	1818 through 1828
Ernst, Daniel	Hanover B.	wagon maker	1833, 1834, 1836, 1837, 1839, 1840
Eshelman, Christian	Washington T.	wagon maker	1820 census
Fetrow, John	Newbury T.	wagon maker	1814 wr, 1816 wr, 1818 wr, 1825 wm, 1828 wm, 1829 wm, 1830 wm, 1831 wm, 1832 wm, 1833 wm, 1834 wm, 1834 farmer, 1835 wm, 1836 farmer, 1837 wm, 1838 farmer
Flanigan, John	Heidelberg T.	wagon maker	1820 census, 1836 wm, 1838 wm
	Hanover B.	wagon maker	1832, 1833, 1834
Ford, Daniel	York B.	wagon maker	1838 wagner, 1840 wm, 1841 wm, 1842 wm, 1843 wm, 1844 wm, 1845 wm
Frysinger, George	Hanover B.	wagon maker	1818 through 1828 wm, 1829 wm & merchant, 1830 wm, 1831 wm, 1832 wm & iron merch. 1836 wm, 1837 wm
Frysinger, Jesse	Hanover B.	wagon maker	1828 through 1837 wm, 1838 coach m, 1839 cm
Ginder, Daniel	Newbury T.	wagon maker	1834
Girk, Francis	Hanover B.	coach maker	1839
Goddart, John	York B.	coach trimmer	1841
Grats, Jacob	Warrington T.	wagon maker	1820 census
Grats, John	Washington T.	wagon maker	1820 census
Grom, David	Hanover B.	wagon maker	1822
Gross, Peter	Dover T.	wagon maker	1820 census
Grove, George	Heidelberg T.	wagon maker	1816
	Hanover B.	wagon maker	1818 through 1833 wm, 1836 wm, 1836 through 1840 cm
Grove, Jacob	Hanover B.	wagon maker	1836 wm, 1836 through 1840 cm

Grove, John	Hanover B.	wagon maker	1831 through 1836 wm, 1837 through 1840 cm
Hamilton, James	York B.	coach maker	1846
Higeman, Peter	Paradise T.	wagon maker	1820 census
Hofman, Adam	Heidelberg T.	wagon maker	1817, 1820 census
Kock, George	York B.	wheelwright	1840
Lanius, Christian	York B.	wagon maker	1809 deed
Leaver, John	Hanover B.	wagon maker	1818, 1822
	York B.	wagon maker	1840
Little, Henry	Hanover B.	wagon maker	1822
Little, Michael	Hanover B.	wagon maker	1822
Lowmaster, Frederick	York B.	wagon maker	1783 deed, died about 1801 (see text)
Lowmaster, Jacob	York B.	wagon maker	born c. 1790, died 1863 (see text)
Mapes, Wm. H.	York B.	coach maker	1843
May, Daniel	Newbury T.	wagon maker	1838, 1839, 1840, 1842, 1845 wr
May, Jacob	Newbury T.	wagon maker	1841 wm, 1844 laborer
May, Jesse	Newbury T.	wagon maker	1846
May, Jonathan	Newbury T.	wheelwright	1818
McFarland, Ambrose	Hanover B.	carriage maker	1836, 1837
McGuire, John	York B.	coach maker	1843 through 1848
McWilliams, James	Hanover B.	wagon maker	1828, 1829
McWilliams, Jesse	Heidelberg T.	wagon maker	1832
Michael, Henry	Hanover B.	wheelwright	1826, 1830
Michael, Lewis	Hanover B.	wheelwright	1832
Michael, William	Hanover B.	wheelwright	1832, 1836, 1837
Miller, Jacob	York B.	wheelwright	1838
Moiers, John	Newbury T.	wagon maker	1837
Morrison, Robert W.	York B.	coach maker	1841
Mummert, Samuel	Paradise T.	wagon maker	1820 census
Myers, David	Hanover B.	wagon maker	1819 innkeeper, iron monger & wagon maker, 1820 wm, 1821 wm, 1822 wm
Myers, John	Newbury T.	wheelwright	1814, 1816, 1817, 1818
Noll, George	Hanover B.	wheelwright	1819, 1826 through 1833, 1836, 1837
Noll, Jacob	Hanover B.	wheelwright	1819
Numbers, Joseph	York B.	coach maker	1840, 1841, 1842, 1844, 1845
Pence, Henry	Newbury T.	wagon maker	1838 through 1841, 1844, 1845, 1846
Phlieger, Adam	York B.	wagon maker	1846, 1847
Potts, Joseph	Newbury T.	wheelwright	1826 wr, 1827 wr, 1828 wr, 1830 chair maker, 1831 chair maker

Price, Horatio	Hanover B.	wagon maker	1829, 1830, 1831
Revert, John	Heidelberg T.	wagon maker	1820 wm, 1836, 1839, 1840
Ruhrer, Jacob	Hanover B.	wagon maker	1831, 1834
Rupp, Christian	York B.	wagon maker	1839 wagner, 1840 wm, 1841 wm, 1842 wm, 1843 wr, 1844 wm, 1845 wm, 1846 wm, 1847 wm, 1848 wm
Schmidt, John	Heidelberg T.	wagon maker	1839, 1841, 1843
Schriner, Lawrence	Heidelberg T.	wagon maker	1822, 1823, 1824, 1829
	Hanover B.	wagon maker	1836
Shannon, John P.	York B.	coach trimmer	1843
Sheffer, Abraham	Dover T.	wagon maker	1820 census
Shetter, George	York B.	auger maker	1838 smith, 1841 auger m, 1842 auger m, 1843 auger m, 1844 smith, 1845 smith, 1846 smith, 1847 smith; earlier he was a wagon maker, and during War of 1812 made cannon carriages & tumbrels; shop sketched by Lewis Miller
Shetter, George Jr.	York B.	auger maker	1838 smith, 1841 auger maker, 1843 auger maker, 1847 smith; he probably worked on wagons with his father
Shock, Benjamin	York B.	coach maker	1841, 1842, 1843
Shrock, Michael	York B.	coach maker	1841, 1842
Stouch, Henry	Dover T.	wagon maker	1820 census
Small, Enos	York B.	coach maker	1838, 1841, 1843, 1844, 1845, 1846, 1847
Small, Joseph	York B.	coach maker	1838, 1841, 1842, 1843 cm on George St., 1847 cm estate
Smith, Alexander	York B.	coach maker	1843
Smith, John	E. Manchester	wagon maker	1820 census
	Hanover B.	wagon maker	1836, 1837
	Heidelberg T.	wagon maker	1844
Soliday, Andrew	Hanover B.	coach maker	1839, 1840
Soovi, Isaac	York B.	coach painter	1841, 1842
Springer, Jacob	Fairview T.	wagon maker	1820 census
Stauffer, Christian	Hanover B.	wagon maker	1832
Stein, Charles W.	Hanover B.	wagon maker	1829
Stock, Henry	Heidelberg T.	wheelwright	1816
Sunday, Jacob	Paradise T.	wagon maker	1820 census
Sunday, Joseph	Paradise T.	wagon maker	1820 census
Sunday, Peter	Paradise T.	wagon maker	1820 census

Taylor, Isaac	Newbury T.	wagon maker	1830, 1832 through 1837 wm, 1838 laborer, 1839 laborer, 1840 laborer, 1842 wm, 1843 farmer, 1844 wm, 1845 farmer
Taylor, John	Newbury T.	wagon maker	1825 through 1834 wm, 1835 stiller
Thompson, Isaac	York B.	coach smith	1843
Updegraff, Joseph	York B.	wagon maker	1838 wagner, 1840 through 1847 wm
Waln, Jonathan	Newbury T.	wheelwright	1814
Wentile, Israel	Fairview T.	wagon maker	1820 census
Wenebrenner, Henry	Heidelberg T.	wheelwright	1816
	Hanover B.	wheelwright	1819, 1820, 1821, 1826, 1827, 1828
Werking, Henry	Heidelberg T.	wagon maker	1820 census, 1823
Wissenall, John	York B.	wagon maker	1841, 1843, 1844
Wonderle, Jacob	Hanover B.	coach trimmer	1836, 1839, 1840
Zeigler, Charles	Hanover B.	wagon maker	1818, 1819, 1822 through 1833, 1836

REFERENCES —

1. Dillin, J. G. W. (1959) *The Kentucky Rifle:* G. Shumway, Publisher, York, Pa.
2. Kindig, Joe, Jr. (1960) *Thoughts on the Kentucky Rifle in its Golden Age:* G. Shumway, Publisher, York, Pa.
3. Kauffman, Henry J. (1960) *The Pennsylvania-Kentucky Rifle:* The Stackpole Press, Harrisburg, Pa.
4. Searight, T. B. (1894) *The Old Pike, A History of the National Road:* T. B. Searight, Pub., Uniontown, Pa.
5. Prowell, George R. (1907) *History of York County, Pennsylvania:* J. H. Beers & Co., Chicago.

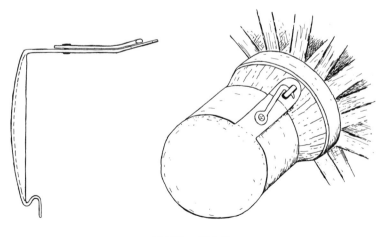

HUB CAP

FIGURE 40. Louis Miller was a carpenter of York, Pa., who delighted in making sketches and drawings of the ordinary happenings around York during the first half of the nineteenth century. Along the border of a more formal drawing he mentions the wagons made in York, shows a hurried sketch of one, and lists the wagon makers and blacksmiths of the town.

Chapter 9

The Conestoga Horse

THE demands for the efficient hauling of freight in early America were so great that there occurred not only the evolution of the Conestoga wagon to carry the freight, but also the evolution of the Conestoga horse to pull the wagon. The Conestoga horse became a recognized American breed in the first half of the nineteenth century, but as the need for long-distance freighting diminished in the second half of the century, so the need for the horse diminished. The breed exists no longer, and our knowledge about it must be taken from early written accounts and drawings.

Large and sturdy draught horses used for pulling Conestoga wagons, and known as Conestoga horses, apparently were in use at the time of the American Revolutionary War. The earliest specific reference to such an animal, of which the writers are aware, is dated 1788, and from the matter-of-fact way in which the animal is mentioned, it seems reasonable to extrapolate its existence back a couple of horse-generations into the Revolutionary period, at least. Pittsburgh had a newspaper, the *Pittsburgh Gazette,* as early as 1786. In the issue for April 26, 1788 the well-known frontier lawyer, Hugh H. Brackenridge, wrote an article chiding the legislators from western Pennsylvania for defeating a bill to provide better roads:

"Perhaps it might be well that the road from Philadelphia to Pittsburgh should remain as it is, because in that case it would resemble the way to Heaven, rough, rugged, and difficult to pass. It may have been for this reason that our western country members, and those of Cumberland especially, holy and religious men, voted against the bill, by which it was proposed to make it good; I mean the bill for laying out one great state road through Carlisle and to the western country, and for expending 2,500£ annually upon it, until it was properly improved.

"The reason assigned is different, viz. that the tax by which this sum was to be raised would be unequal: A tax upon horses, in which case a western country horse would pay as much as a horse below, a Conestoga one for instance; though a western country horse is not of the same value with a Conestoga horse, that is to do the argument justice his use of labor is not of equal value, because the produce of the toil on which he is employed is not of such value. . . .

"I am of the opinion, that whatever asses may think, were it left to the Westmoreland horse himself, he would determine that though he might pay a little more of his tax than came to his share, yet he would make it up in the wear and tear of hoof, which he would save by coming across the mountains on a good road; either as a pack horse, in a waggon, or with a rider on his back. I am convinced that if those in the negative to this bill had possessed the feeling of horses, even without the sense, they would have reasoned in the same manner. As for that texi-pedegogue (sic) creature, who has advanced that kind of argument, he shows himself in this, as in all other cases of politics, to draw his ideas from his own circumstances and situation of life. When he looked at his low pony that he rods, and compared it with the big Conestoga horse, he thought it hard that poor Snaffle should pay as much as Granby, and so voted against the bill. . ."

A year later, in 1789, Dr. Benjamin Rush wrote that it was no uncommon sight to see 100 wagons a day, carrying merchandise from the Dutch settlements to Philadelphia, each drawn by four or five horses of a "peculiar breed," undoubtedly Conestogas.[1] In the same account Rush commented on the especially large size of the horses owned by the German peoples of early Pennsylvania.

The subject of the Conestoga horse was studied extensively by Dr. Herbert H. Beck (1875-1960), of Lancaster.[2] The earliest reference he could find to the name "Conestoga horse" was published in 1832. Under the heading of the "American Horse" the 1832 writer recognized three breeds, the Canadian, the English, and the Conestoga. He wrote:[3] "The Conestoga Horse is found in Pennsylvania and the Middle States, and is long in limb, and light in carcass, sometimes rising 17 hands."

A brief description of the horse was given by I. Daniel Rupp in 1842:[4] "The Conestoga Horse — This horse is found in Pennsylvania and the Middle States. He is generally long in leg, and rather light in the carcass; sometimes seventeen hands and a half height—he is used for the plough and carriage—he is an excellent carriage horse. Those of middle size, when well made, are much used for the saddle, and are useful for hunting." He presented an illustration of this horse, which is reproduced here (FIG. 41), and captioned it "A Lancaster County Draft Horse."

Probably the most comprehensive contemporary account of the Conestoga horse is found in a report of the U. S. Department of Agriculture for 1863, written by Honorable John Strohm (1793-1884) of Lancaster County. Some selected passages from this report follow:[5]

"The wide celebrity acquired by this distinguished animal has induced the belief that he springs from some peculiar species or breed of that genus of quadrupeds whose services contribute so largely to the comfort and prosperity of man, especially in an agricultural community. And it has inspired a desire to know something about the origin, comparitive merits, and system of breeding, of a class of horses whose fame is commensurate with a large portion of the United States.

"I am fully impressed with the belief that the superior excellence attributed to the Conestoga horse is not derived from any strain or breed that can now be traced to its origin. The following sketch has been penned with the view of exploding that idea, and at the same time to rescue the history of that celebrated animal from that oblivion to which modern innovations are rapidly consigning him.

"The name of 'Conestoga' is derived from a river . . . that rises in the northeast part of the county of Lancaster, . . . The river rises in, and flows through a region of country of unsurpassed fertility, where cereal grains and nutritious grasses are grown to an extent unrivalled in any part of the United States.

"The settlement of this valley commenced in the early part of the last century (about 1725). The first European settlers emigrated mainly from Switzerland and the adjoining parts of Germany, interspersed with French Huguenots. They were principally agriculturists, and from necessity as well as choice, devoted their attention to the same vocation in their new home.

"Their first care was to clear the ground of the heavy timber growth that extended over the whole region. Their next object was to break up the ground, and prepare it for the reception of the seed, from which the abundant harvest was anticipated.

"In the accomplishment of this, the horse was found a useful and convenient, if not indispensable assistant. For without the aid of this useful animal the cultivation of the soil must have been very limited. The horses used by those early settlers were no doubt the progenitors of the far-famed 'Conestoga horse', which in after times became so extensively known and spoken of. But of what particular stock or strain they were, or whence they came, history and tradition are equally silent, or afford no reliable information.

"As Chester County and the vicinity of Philadelphia were partially settled and considerably improved before any settlement was effected in the Conestoga valley, it is quite probable that the first immigrants to this valley derived their first stock of horses from their nearest neighbors, inhabiting the above named localities. And it requires no great streach of the imagination to suppose that the first settlers of Pennsylvania who came here with William Penn, or some of their immediate successors, brought some of those useful animals with them from England, from which the whole stock of horses in the country at that time were derived.

"But it was not only in the cultivation of the soil that the horse was so essential to the immigrants to this (then new) country. There being then no flouring mills in the county of Lancaster, the inhabitants were compelled to carry their grain to the Brandywine mills, near Wilmington, Delaware, some forty miles distant, to be manufactured into flour for family use.

"This was a laborous task that could hardly have been executed without the aid of the useful animal that forms the subject of this essay. Just, humane and generous, this rural people treated this trusty and faithful domestic with a degree of consideration seldom bestowed upon any of the brute creation.

"Being thus well fed, protected from the cold and inclemency of the weather when not actually in service, and never overworked or abused, this horse, under this kind treatment attained to the full development of his natural powers. He arrived at a degree of beauty and perfection seldom found in any other country, and much surpassing the original stock. The deep interest with which the farmers of this region regarded this noble animal, naturally stimulated a desire to improve the stock and to bring him to a still greater degree of perfection.

"This was not attempted by any scientific system of breeding; for this frugal people, always having an eye to economy and utility, kept neither males nor females for the exclusive purpose of breeding. Sometimes a stud horse was absolved from labor during the last months of spring and the first of the summer season; but at the ex-

piration of that term he was put to the harness again and compelled
to do his share of the labor which the interest of his proprietor required. So with the mare; she was generally worked until within a
few weeks of foaling. In about a week after the mare had foaled she
was again put to the harness and performed her ordinary share of
labor on the farm. The colt was permitted to run with its dam until
it was about three months old; then it was weaned and turned to
pasture.

"At about two and a half years old they were usually 'bridle broken'
and sometimes lightly worked for a while in the autumn. But during
the ensuing winter they were commonly suffered to run idle, being
seldom regularly worked until fully three years old.

"Under this system of breeding, by selecting their best stock for
the purpose, the farmers of the Conestoga valley were very successful
in improving their stock. As the country was brought under cultivation, and the dense forest was succeeded by fertile fields, roads were
opened and facilities afforded for transporting the surplus produc-
tions of the farm to the seaboard. Wagons were now introduced (for
railroads and canals were not then in vogue), and the strength and
fidelity of the horse were relied upon to drag those heavy-laden wagons to their destined places.

"In the performance of those services it will readily be perceived
that strength and activity were the most essential requisites. To these
points then, the attention of the sagacious farmer was constantly directed, in the improvement of this indispensable quadruped. The aim
being to produce a strong, heavy, well-set, and tolerably active animal, with great powers of endurance.

"The immigration to and settling of the western states created a
demand for the transportation of large quantities of dry goods and
groceries to supply the wants of those engaged in opening up and
settling those new countries. Many of the farmers in the Conestoga
valley occasionally employed their teams in hauling 'store goods'
from Philadelphia to Pittsburg, the latter place being the terminus
beyond which the eastern teams seldom went.

"During the War of 1812 these noble teams rendered essential
service to the country in the transportation of arms, ammunition and
supplies to the army of the frontier. Long lines of those teams were
frequently seen wending their weary way to the theatre of action, and
contributed greatly to the comfort of the army and the defense of the

country. Their usual route of travel was from Philadelphia through Lancaster, crossing the Susquehanna at Columbia or Marietta, and thence over the mountains to Pittsburg, and sometimes northward to Lake Erie.

"The Conestoga horse, then, though his origin cannot be traced to a distinct species or breed, though his pedigree is not recorded in any stud-book or his exploits blazoned forth on the pages of a turf-register, is still not a myth. He is not the creature of a fervid imagination or a disordered fancy—but a veritable, strong, active animal, pre-eminently useful in his day and generation, brought to perfection by judicious breeding, kind treatment and careful management.

"From the preceeding considerations, I come to the conclusion that the Conestoga horse is not a distinct strain of that noble quadruped, but belongs to a class that has attained a great degree of efficiency for a particular purpose. And that the appellation by which this class is so widely known denotes superior excellence in the class of draught horses, although the individuals composing it may have sprung from a crossing or mixture of various breeds or families into which the horse family is at present divided.

"There is, however, one distinguishing characteristic in the history of this animal that has been but slightly adverted to, which perhaps deserves a more extended notice. That is the high condition in which the animal is usually kept in the region of country from which he derives his name and his fame.

"The farmers of the Conestoga valley, as a general rule, are in the habit of feeding more grain to their horses and keeping them in higher condition than those of any other section of country, known to the writer of this article. Indeed, the keeping of very fat horses has become a passion with them.

"I do not mean to intimate, however, that every fat horse is a Conestoga horse. But I never knew that flattering term to be applied to a lean, gaunt, half-starved-looking animal, whatever his merits, good points, or other qualifications may have been. Hence we frequently hear such expressions as 'broad as a Conestoga horse', 'fat as a Conestoga horse', 'has a neck (or breast) like a Conestoga stallion', used either in compliment, irony, or derision, according to the humor or design of the speaker."

Dr. H. H. Beck, writing in 1941, gives an account of a particularly large Conestoga horse:[2] "Henry H. Snavely, of Lititz, who was born in 1858, is one of the local few [left with personal memories of the Conestoga horse]. He was born on a farm near Oregon, Manheim Township, and he has been a horseman all his life. He says the Conestoga horse was the common talk among the older horsemen of his youth. He well remembers a famous Conestoga horse, known by that name, on the neighboring farm of John Shirk. This was between 1870 and 1875. He says this horse was considerably taller than the other farm horses, well over seventeen hands, and weighed over 1,800 pounds. It was a white-faced bay with one glass eye. It was long legged, not chunky. It was notable for its pulling strength. Mr. Snavely well remembers a wager, the talk of the country at the time, which was taken by John Shirk. It was that the white-faced bay could pull three tons from Lancaster to the farm near Oregon. Mr. Shirk won the bet."

Beck concludes his writing with the following summary:[2] "With all breeding records lost, probably because they were never written, the original blood lines of the so-called Conestoga horse are conjectural and must always remain so. However, from legendary accounts as well as the general conformation and character of the animal, as described by earlier horsemen and remembered by men still living, it is a fair surmise that the Conestoga horse, which of course was subject to minor variations, as all breeds are, collectively was the outcome of breeding Flemish or similar imported draught horses, like the famous Suffolk Punch of England, with lighter boned, higher blooded stock identical with or similar to the thoroughbred of today. Improvement within the established breed to high, though doubtless quite variable standards, was then the result of careful feeding, stabling and general handling and the selection of the best of the sires in the immediate neighborhood. For about a century Conestoga was a name applied over the general range of Pennsylvania and neighboring states to a type of horse best adapted to pulling heavy loads over long, rough and hilly roads.

"An analysis of the data on the animal would indicate that the Conestoga horse, in general, was usually a bay of a black, rather long of leg, muscular but not chunky, with a fairly small head and arched crest. It was well mannered and it had enormous pulling strength. Its average height was 16.3 hands; its average weight 1650 pounds."

In writing about the Conestoga horse in 1955, Albert I. Drachman utilized the findings and observations of the earlier writers to point out that even after a recognizable type came into being in the early nineteenth century, its development continued throughout the wagoning era:[6]

"The first point that needs to be emphasized is this: The Conestogas *were never a real breed* in the true sense of the word. They were verging toward becoming one, with characteristics gradually growing more uniform and fixed, toward the large and heavy draft type.

"If allowed to continue developing along this line, they would undoubtedly have become a genuine breed, relatively invariable and breeding true. The spreading of the canal and railroad systems, which made these heavy freight movers unnecessary, put an end to their development before that stage in their evolution was reached.

"This makes comprehensible the differing descriptions of the animals. The type being not yet standardized, different individuals would vary, both within a community, and from locality to locality. In those days, within each small area, some one, or a few desirable prepotent stallions would be bred to the local mares. The traits of the sires would be handed on to their get, and as the latter matured and were bred in their turn, would tend to characterize the horses of that district. Thus the qualities would vary from place to place.

"Aside from the variations with space, just indicated, there was also notable differentiation with time. The earlier accounts, the ones of the *Lancaster Horse* period, describe the animal as light, long-legged, active and suitable for road work under saddle or hitched to carriages.

"The later descriptions stress size, weight and the great loads that they were able to draw. Thus in the 1870's a Conestoga horse once won a wager for its owner by pulling a weight of three tons for a substantial distance.

"This also ties in with the contradictory statements regarding breeding. Various authors ascribe the Conestoga horse to different progenitors. Each may be correct, at least to this extent: that the source proposed by him did play a part in establishing the type. But on the other hand, any of the writers would be in error if he maintained that his proposed origin is the sole, or almost the sole source of the animals. For undoubtedly these celebrated horses resulted from the mingling of many blood lines.

"From the point of view of time, the so-called Lancaster Horse (FIG. 41), of the period from the late 18th century up to the early

1840's, was the precursor of the final, typical, and more perfect Conestoga. At the first stage the animal was beginning to become heavier, but still showed many of the traits of the lighter breeds—alert, long, relatively thin-limbed, apparently active and spirited.

"When the later and really massive type of Conestoga wagon was developed, and the transportation of large volumes of freight became an extensive activity, the need for heavier horses was apparent. The animals could now be profitably specialized for that purpose, leaving the saddle and light carriage duties to other types.

"The production of heavier horses was stimulated, resulting in animals like that in [FIGURE 42], with its larger head, greater chunkiness, shorter and thicker legs, and other typical draft characteristics. These include calmness, placidity, and a quiet reserve of power, ready for use when needed, but not wasted in needless tension, activity, or unnecessary movements. Their average weights seem to have been between 1600 and 1700 lbs. in their final developed form."

Another illustration of a "Conestoga draught-horse" (FIG. 43) was published in London in 1869[5]. This horse differs hardly at all from the one shown in the 1863 U. S. Department of Agriculture publication (FIG. 42).

REFERENCES —

1. Rush, Dr. Benjamin (1910) *An Account of the Manners of the German Inhabitants of Pennsylvania:* Pennsylvania-German Society, Lancaster, Pa.
2. Beck, Herbert H. (1941) Conestoga Horse, Pioneer in Pennsylvania Transportation: Penna. Dept. of Internal Affairs, Monthly Bulletin, in three parts.
3. Doughty, J. & H. (pub.) (1832) *The Cabinet of Natural History and American Rural Sports:* J. & H. Doughty, Philadelphia.
4. Rupp, I. Daniel (1842) *The Farmer's Complete Farrier:* Gilbert Hills, Lancaster, Pa.
5. Strom, John (1863) The Conestoga Horse, in *Report of the Commissioner of Agriculture for the Year 1863:* Government Printing Office, Washington.
6. Drachman, Albert I. (1955) The Conestoga Horse, *The Pennsylvania Dutchman,* v. VI, no. 4.

Chapter 10
The Team and its Control

by Albert I. Drachman

THE method of driving a Conestoga team was remarkable, for the six powerful animals and the long wagon behind them were managed by a driver holding one single line called the *jerk line* (FIG. 44, FIG. 45). Moreover, this seemingly inadequate means of control was further diluted by the line being connected to the bit of just one of the horses, the nigh (near) leader or left front horse, commonly called simply *the leader*. In horseman's language *near* means *left,* and *off* means *right.*

Normally in driving stage coaches and almost all vehicles except Conestoga wagons, a pair of divided lines is used for each pair of horses abreast—two lines for a two-horse team and six lines for six animals. This gives the driver contact with each side of each horse's bit, and direct control over all six of the team.

But how could a single line hitched only to the left front horse be used to turn all six animals to the right, or to stop them? In the first place, heavy draft horses are naturally docile; Conestoga horses were decidedly so. They were also thoroughly trained, accustomed to human handling, and never subjected to fast work or other exciting treatment. In addition, their training included responding to the voice. The word *haw* meant *turn left,* the word *gee* (often pronounced *yee* or *yay* meant *turn right,* and of course *whoa* meant *stop.*

Without mentioning it further it should be understood in the remainder of this explanation that the vocal command, with or without line signal, should invariably be given whenever any response from the team is desired. As my friend, the present day Conestoga wagoner Elmer D. Lapp says, "A good leader you just speak to; a line is for safety first."

The Jerk Line

The long single jerk line is divided into branches which pass on either side of the leader's neck and fasten to opposite sides of the bit (FIG. 46). These two branches are known as the *lead rein* (in the singular). The right branch is adjusted from half an inch to an inch longer than the left. Thus, when the driver gives a medium gentle pull, only the left branch is tightened enough to act on the bit, and the horse turns in that direction. So far this is direct control.

Turning to the right is slightly more involved. The driver gives a number of short, quick jerks on the line. This tightens the off branch sufficiently that the animal now feels the bit jerking on his right, and turns to that side. Of course he feels it also on his near side, but he has been thoroughly trained that jerks mean *turn to the right*. Though horses are not intelligent reasoners, they do learn remarkably well by association, have excellent memories, and are creatures of habit. Either the word *gee* or jerks on the bit would mean the same. The leader has here a doubly reinforced association which he remembers well, and to which he habitually responds by turning right.

To stop, the word *whoa* usually suffices. If the animals combine the halt with something of an undesired turn to right or left, the driver corrects it by the appropriate signal to the opposite side. If they do not completely halt, a judicious combination of pulls and jerks with repetition of the *whoa* will obtain compliance.

So much for the leader. But the driver has no contact with the bits of the rest of the team. How then does he control them? Horses are herd animals, and except for a few individuals, the "nature of the beast" is to be a follower. Before his young stock is two years old, a Conestoga wagoner usually can tell which colt to train as leader. The others are followers.

To this natural instinct of his animals the driver adds two simple devices to assure conformity. The first is a short pair of reins for each horse of the team (not shown in FIGURES 44, and 45), forming a V shape similar to the leader's lead rein. One end of each is connected to the left side, and one to the right side of each animal's bit. The point of each V, however, is hooked behind the animal's collar, instead of to the jerk line. This allows reasonable swaying and nodding of the horses' heads, but restricts excessive motion. Thus, even though the driver holds no lines to those horses, each animal is conscious of the restraining influence of bit and reins.

The Jockey Stick

The second, and more direct control of the other horses is by means of the jockey stick (FIG. 46). This is a light but firm rod, one end of which is fastened to the leader's collar, and the other end hung loosely from the off side of his right hand mate's bit. Thus, without unduly hampering the off leader's head movements, it nevertheless gives direct signals to his sensitive mouth, reproducing the leader's motions. When the neigh leader starts, stops, turns left or right, his mate simply must do the same. The middle pair and the wheelers, obeying their natural instinct, follow the leaders. In fact, hemmed in between leaders and the wagon, it would be very difficult physically for them not to do so.

To keep the jerk line from drooping toward the ground, it is passed through three large rings, one attached to the leader's hip, a second attached to the swing leader's hame, and the third attached to the swing leader's hip (Fig. 44). It is important to note that these large rings had about a dozen little rings (preferably brass) on each of them, so that a pull or jerk on the line caused them to jingle. This sound was unlike the bell sound, and thus was distinguishable to all the horses' ears.

This jingling of the little rings on the big ring acted as a signal to all horses to start pulling. While the voice of the teamster usually started the horses pulling (and not all teamsters had a good teamster voice), the jerk line jingling of these rings meant to all team horses "Start to pull." The mere motion of the line was sufficient to start them without the use of the voice. Sometimes this was show-off, or substitution for a poor teamster voice. Heavy loads were more easily started by a series of right and left swinging of the team, to move the front wheels before starting up the whole load.

Training the Leader

So far it has been explained how six *trained* horses can be driven with only one line. Training a leader becomes the most important part of training a team. This apparently difficult feat of training is accomplished by means which, though difficult to imagine in advance, are relatively simple.

In training a leader, the driver holds in his hand a jerk line hooked up in the regular manner. But in addition, for training purposes only, he holds in his right hand a long line snapped onto the *right* side of the bit. While the colt is walking, the trainer calls out *haw* and gives a steady, light pull with his left hand. This transmits a direct pull to the animal's mouth, and he turns left.

To train the colt to turn right, the man calls *gee,* jerks the line in his left hand a few times, and simultaneously gives a steady pull on the line in his right hand. At this stage of his training, the jerks and the oral command would mean nothing more to the animal than a mild annoyance, but the direct pull from the training line turns him to the right.

Similarly, to train the colt to stop, the driver calls out *whoa* and gives a steady pull on both lines. It is the pull which stops the animal. But if the trainer never omits the vocal signal, it will not be long before the word alone will make the colt halt. Once the stop, the right turn, and the left turn have been thoroughly learned, and associated with their respective signals, the extra lines can be discarded. Thereafter the horse is controlled with nothing more than voice, assisted when necessary by the jerk line.

In actual practice, the leaders of wagon teams were usually trained by farmers. Ordinarily one of the smaller intelligent horses was selected for this training. The larger ones were used at the tongue of the wagon. After the simple preliminary training was completed, as explained above, the best place to thoroughly accustom a leader to a jerk line was in ploughing. The lead horse followed the furrow, and the other horses were caused to follow him by means of the jockey stick.

At the end of the row the left turn was simple. But if the farmer wished his leader to turn to the right, he threw the plow around by hand, then walked to the head of the leader, gave short jerks on the lead rein with his right hand, and pushed the horse's head to the right with his left hand. This process was repeated until the animal became accustomed to the use of the jerk line. Many hundreds of right and left turns were made in the course of a week's plowing. After a horse became a perfect leader in the plowing process, he went on the road as a leader of a four, five or six horse hitch-up.

Sometimes when a new leader was to be broken beside an old leader, they were hitched side by side, without jockey stick, and a jerk line attached to each. The driver thus could pull or jerk both lines simultaneously. The student animal instinctively would follow the old leader, and learn the feeling of the bit. Before long he would associate correctly right turns with jerking, and left turns with a direct pull.

Chapter 11
Harnesses and Accessories

IN THE 1863 Report of the U. S. Department of Agriculture, John Strohm wrote as follows:[1]

"The wagoners of the Conestoga century seemed to be fully aware of and to appreciate the importance of their teams. They evinced considerable taste and no little pride in the style of fitting them out. The harness was constructed of the best materials, with an eye to show as well as utility. In the harness and trimmings of these teams they frequently indulged in expenses that approached extravagance. In addition to what was indispensably necessary, articles that by some were deemed mere decorations were sometimes appended. Attached to their noble animals, these served to further increase the admiration which they so universally attracted.

"It was, indeed, an animating sight to see five or six highly fed horses, half covered with heavy bear skins, or decorated with gaudily fringed housings, surmounted with a set of finely toned bells, their bridles adorned with loops of red trimming, and moving over the ground with a brisk elastic step, snorting disdainfully at surrounding objects, as if half conscious of their superior appearance, and participating in the pride that swelled the bosom of their master and driver."

One hundred and one years have passed since Strohm's moving description of a team in harness was published. The horse and wagon era continued throughout the second half of the nineteenth century and on into the twentieth century, but now even this is about two generations down the road of history. Everyday words of a few generations ago, like trace, hame, collar, and housing may be unfamiliar to many readers, so a brief description of some of these items may be useful for understanding the Conestoga harness.

The pulling force of a horse is exerted on a wagon by means of the traces, which are chains, or heavy leather straps, that fasten to the singletree (FIG. 45). The singletree is a piece of wood a little longer than a horse is wide, about 32 inches long, that has a hook at either end for a trace to fasten to, and an eye in the center to fasten it in turn to the doubletree. There are a pair of traces for each horse, and these run along each side of the horse and fasten to the hames. The hames consist of a pair of curved pieces of wood that are linked top and bottom, and these fit against the outside of the collar and fasten to it. The collar essentially is a pad that makes it possible for a horse to exert his pulling force against the hames without being discomforted. The housing is a wide piece of leather that rests on top of the hame and collar assembly.

The harness used on the pole or wheel horses was much heavier than that of the leaders and swing leaders (FIG. 46). The backing bands or breeching of this heavy "breechband" harness often were six inches wide and the hip straps equally wide. The traces were made of leather four or five inches wide, with short iron chain traces next to the singletrees. These iron traces were chains of short links, with longer links at the end where they hooked to the leather traces for adjustment as to length. At the outer end of the leather trace were three or four long links to make adjustment at the hames.

The harness of the leaders and swing leaders were the same, essentially, but differed markedly from the "breechband" harness of the pole horses (FIG. 48). This harness, called front gears, consisted of a heavy leather saddle strap eight to ten inches wide and highly ornamented with sewing, which carried the traces, and a bellyband two or more inches wide. It had a hip strap three or four inches wide, and contained a crupper. The traces for these horses were made entirely of chain, in short links, but with a few long links for adjustment, and they extended all the way from the hames to the single trees. If the traces were too long, knots were tied in them close to the singletrees.

The hames usually were made from white oak wood taken from the roots of white oak stumps that conformed to the shape of a hame. These hames, with the grain of the wood running their full length, were especially strong and tough. At a much later period sawed hames came into use. Near the top of each hame were two staples into which one prong of the bell frame was inserted.

Collars were made entirely of leather, and were fastened at the top by means of a strap and buckle. A denim-covered collar with a patented fastener came into use in the late days of wagoning.

The housings used for teaming were made very wide and long in order to protect the horse's shoulders from the weather. The ends of the housings extended down over the traces, thus practically keeping the entire shoulder and neck dry in wet weather. There was no better place for the saddler to show his artistry than on these large housings. He often decorated them with ornamental stitching and design sewing. In later years brass studs were added for ornamental purposes, but the Conestoga wagon saddler stuck largely to plain leather housings. These large leather housings were warm for a horse, so for farm work or for short hauls, where horses were exposed to the weather for only a short time, a smaller housing, or no housing at all, was used.

The bridle accessory to the large Conestoga wagon gear was the one-piece bridle with big blinders and a wide nose and forehead piece, all cut from one piece of leather. The throat latch and bit straps were extra, of course, but the major portion of the bridle was made from one leather piece. The bridles were so highly ornamented with ribbons, sometimes, that large portions of the bridle were covered entirely.

The jerk line was more than twenty five feet long, extending from the lead horse to the wagon brake. A slit was cut in the line by the saddler, and by this means the line could be hung over the hame of the saddle horse so that it was easily accessible when the teamster either rode or walked. Special leather was selected for the line and in many cases it was two inches or more in width so that there was slight possibility of its breaking.

The spreader, with its ornate hooks, and the fifth chain, was required for a six-horse team hitch-up. The earliest spreaders were made of wood, later metal fittings were put on their ends, then metal strappings, and finally all-metal spreaders were used. The fifth chain was about ten feet long, made of hand-forged links. Its purpose was to be the effective connection between the two lead horses and the front end of the wagon tongue. Considerable work went into the forging of a fifth chain, and one of the writers (HCF) purchased one of these chains from an octogenarian who vowed that his grandfather paid a blacksmith twenty dollars to make it more than a century before.

The Conestoga wagoner frequently rode in preference to walking beside his wagon, but he rode one of the horses of his team rather than riding on the wagon. The left wheel horse carried an unusual saddle, known as a wagoner's saddle (FIG. 51). It was made on a wooden frame, which was covered with thick leather. This saddle had long

A LANCASTER COUNTY DRAFT HORSE

FIGURE 41. The earliest known illustration of a Conestoga horse is this, published in 1842 in *The Farmer's Complete Farrier*, by I. Daniel Rupp. This long-legged horse is typical for the period from the late 18th century up to the early 1840's.

FIGURE 42. A Conestoga horse in its final stage of development, owned by Calvin Eshelman of Lancaster County, Pa., in 1863; height 16 hands, weight 1350 pounds. This particular animal is relatively small, for the typical Conestoga horse had a weight between 1600 and 1700 pounds. *From the Report of the Commissioner of Agriculture, Washington, D. C., 1863.*

CONESTOGA DRAUGHT-HORSE.

FIGURE 43. A Conestoga draught-horse of the mid-nineteenth century, when its development was in its final form. This illustration was taken from *The Horse in Stable and Field, by Stonehenge, London, 1869.*

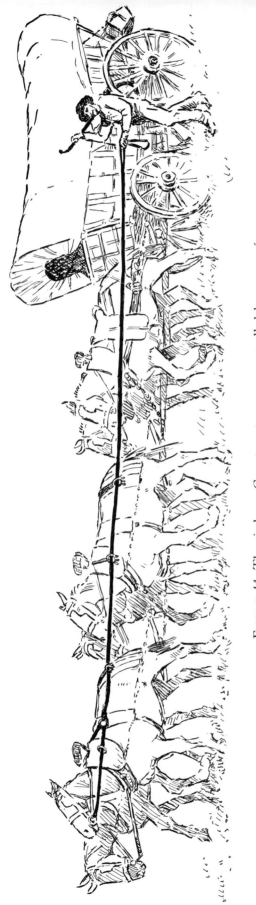

FIGURE 44. The six-horse Conestoga team was controlled by means of a single rein called the jerk line. The driver walked beside the wagon, on the left side, or rode in a saddle mounted on the left rear, or left wheel horse.

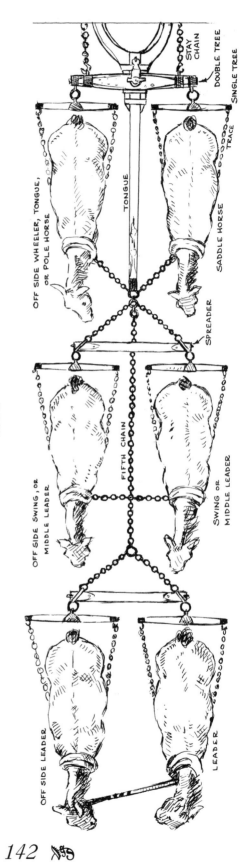

FIGURE 45. The pulling force of a Conestoga team is transmitted to the wagon by means of the traces, single trees, spreaders, fifth chain, and double tree. The stay chains are kept slack, but one side will tighten if the double tree becomes unbalanced too far.

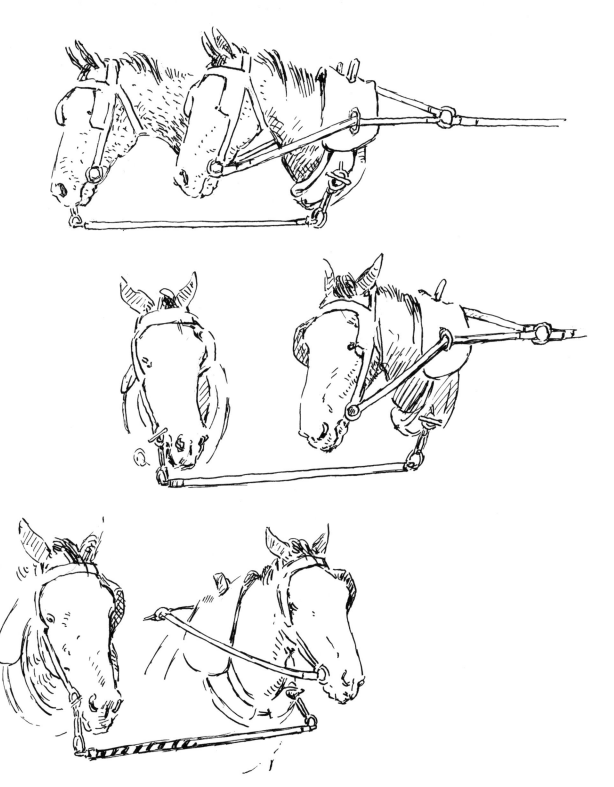

FIGURE 46. Gear for controlling the lead horses of a Conestoga team. The jerk line terminated at the doubled lead rein of the left front horse, of nigh leader. His movements were transmitted to the off leader by means of the jockey stick running from the nigh leader's collar to the off leader's bit.

143

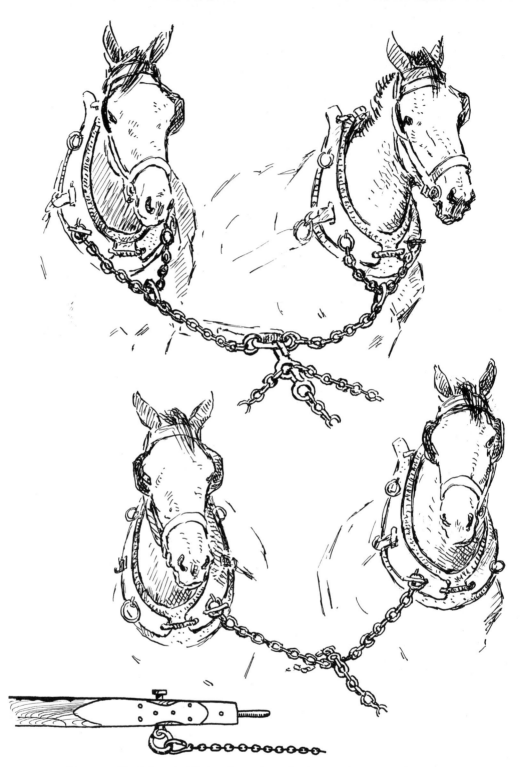

FIGURE 47. (above) Chains kept the pole horses from straying away from the wagon tongue. (below) The middle horses were connected by a chain called the fifth chain carrier which kept them together and which supported the fifth chain. Sometimes the fifth chain was attached to the pole by means of a ring fastened underneath it about 15 inches from the end.

FIGURE 48. A present day Conestoga team in harness. This outfit is owned by John E. Fox of Bernville, Bucks Co., Pa., who brought it to the Pennsylvania Dutch Folk Festival at Kutztown for a number of years in the 1950's.

FIGURE 49. Harness used on the pole or wheel horses of a Conestoga wagon. The wide leather traces can be seen running from the hames to the chains at the bottom. This is one harness of a complete set of six well-preserved specimens on exhibit at the Shelburne Museum, Shelburne, Vt. *Photo by Einars J. Mengis, Shelburne Museum, Inc.*

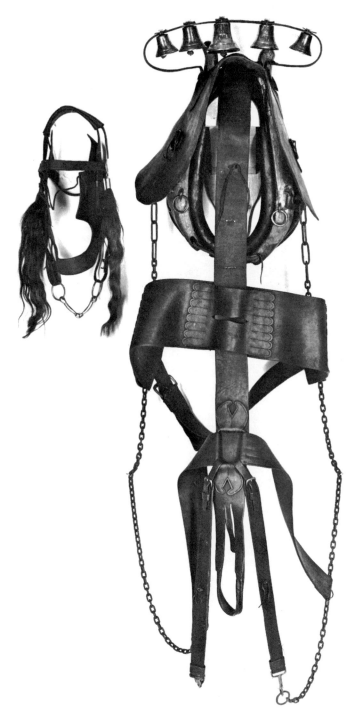

FIGURE 50. Harness used on the lead horses and on the middle horses of a Conestoga team. This is one harness of a complete set of six well-pre-served specimens on exhibit at the Shelburne Museum, Shelburne, Vt.
Photo by Einars J. Mengis, Shelburne Museum, Inc.

FIGURE 51. The saddle of the Conestoga wagoner was simple, and of a special design suited to his purposes. This typical old specimen is in the collection of the Shelburne Museum, in Vermont. *Photo by Einars J. Mengis, Shelburne Museum, Inc.*

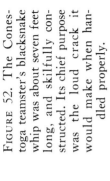

FIGURE 52. The Conestoga teamster's blacksnake whip was about seven feet long, and skilfully constructed. Its chief purpose was the loud crack it would make when handled properly.

FIGURE 53. This octette, the Singing Teamsters, was organized in 1936 to sing the songs, and to help perpetuate the lore, of the long gone Conestoga wagoners. Their first appearance was at the Pennsylvania State Folk Festival, held at Bucknell University in 1936.

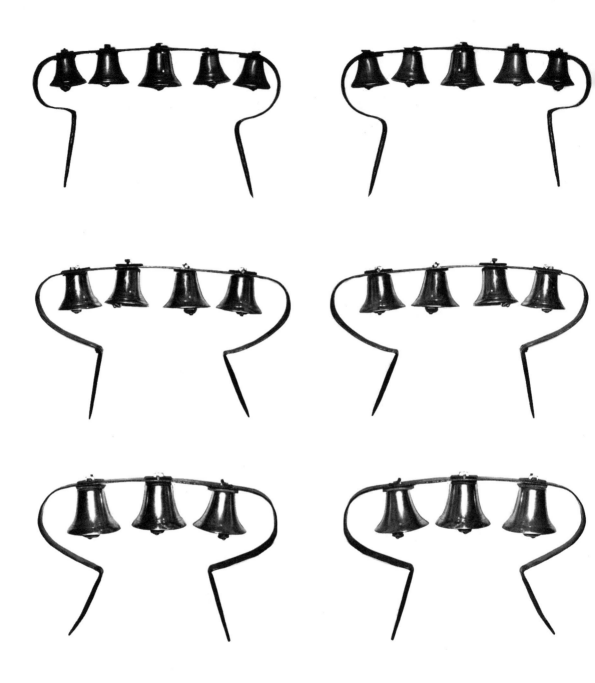

FIGURE 54. A set of bells for a six horse Conestoga team. It was customary for the lead horses to use the arches containing five bells, the middle horses the four-bell arches, and the wheel horses the three-bell arches.

wide skirts with square ends. There was no saddle horn nor pommel, and the cantle was low and sometimes brass-bound. The stirrups were the open type, made of forged iron artistically scrolled and large enough to engage a heavy stogey shoe. In the later years of wagoning it was found that the metal stirrup was dangerous in the event of a fall, and it was superseded by the closed type of wooden stirrup. The Conestoga wagoner's saddle continued to be used as a part of American wagon gear long after the Conestoga days were over. In a harness and saddlery catalog of about 1920 a wagon saddle of the Conestoga type is illustrated.[2]

The blacksnake whip was an indispensable part of every wagoner's equipment. It was about seven feet long, thick and hard at the butt, and tapered to the small end. It terminated with a plaited lash about eighteen inches long, to which a cracker of silk or eelskin was attached. The main portion of the whip was made from one piece of leather and it had but one long seam which was so skillfully done as to be almost invisible. The handle of the whip usually was marked with bands of plaited leather or leather bands ornamented with small brass studs. A strap was sewn to the butt to hang up the whip when it was not in use.

One variety of whip was made with a rawhide interior. Another style was known among the wagoners as a "Louden whip" because it was manufactured in the village of Fort Louden (Franklin Co., Pa.), on the wagon road to Pittsburgh. This whip had an elastic wooden stock and was so popular that it was used almost exclusively by the regular Pitt wagoners on the Philadelphia-Pittsburgh turnpike, and to a limited extent on the National Road. A number of whip makers also worked in the town of York, Pennsylvania.[3]

Bridle rosettes as used on carriage and stage coach horses were varied in design and quite showy, but those used by the Conestoga and Pitt teamsters usually were plain brass buttons.

Tassels, consisting of a bunch of horsehair or wool six to ten inches in length and dyed a vermillion red or pale blue, were fastened by wire or by a leather strap to the bridle under the rosette and dangled at the side of the horse's head. Sometimes these tassels were much longer than ten inches, and were dyed several colors.

Pompons sometimes adorned the strap of the bridle that crossed over the top of the horse's head, and sometimes one or more pompons appeared on top of the bell arches. Colored ribbons were wrapped around the forehead and nose pieces of the bridle, and not infrequently the hair of the horse's forelock was plaited and bedecked with ribbons of red, white, and blue. Such ribbons sometimes were wrapped around the iron bell arch also.

The use of bells on the horses of a Conestoga team was a traditional and sentimental touch which probably had its origins in Europe. Bells have been used for parade purposes for centuries, and in America they commonly were used on pack horses throughout the eighteenth century. Orme's journal mentions the bells of pack horses in the Braddock campaign being muffled during the day but loosened at night.[4] It is not known when bells were first used on Conestoga horses, and it is possible that their use did not develop until the nineteenth century. Pennsylvania tradition would have us believe that bells were commonly used on Pennsylvania teams, but Searight states that on the National Road in the period 1820-1850 bell teams were rare among the many teams on the road.[5]

The Conestoga bell arch was a sturdy piece of wrought iron sixteen to twenty inches across at its widest point (FIG. 54). The bells of brass were fastened beneath this iron arch, and were either three, four, or five, in number. The lead horses frequently carried five relatively small bells on their arches, the middle horses four bells on their arches, and the pole horses three bells of still larger size. The bells were of cast brass, finished by turning, and almost always carry no marks of identification, so it is not known whether they were made in America or imported. On any given arch the bells usually differed in size, so even with matched pairs of arches, there was a potential for twelve different bell tones.

The chiming of a bell team was a grand sound, and the teamsters took great pride in their bells. Some wagoners were so proud of their bells that they tuned them by filing, if they did not sound just right to their critical ears.

There was a well established custom in the days of Conestoga wagoning, that if a teamster was so unfortunate as to get his wagon stuck or mired so as to require the help of another passing teamster, he would have to forfeit his bells. To arrive at the destination without bells was a disgrace which hurt both the pride and the pocket book. From this early custom we have the fine American expression, "I'll be there with bells on." It is said that sometimes a teamster whose wagon was stuck would break his wagon tongue intentionally rather than allow another wagoner to extricate him and claim the prized bells.

REFERENCES —

1. Strohm, John (1863) The Conestoga Horse, in *Report of the Commissioner of Agriculture for the Year 1863:* Government Printing Office, Washington.
2. Perkins-Campbell Co. (c1920) General Catalogue No. 35 Harness, Horse Collars, Saddles and Accessories for the Saddlery Trade: The Perkins-Campbell Co., Cincinnati, Ohio.
3. York Borough, York Co., Pa., property tax records 1800-1850.
4. Sargent, Winthrop (1855) *The History of an Expedition Against Fort Duquesne:* Philadelphia.
5. Searight, T. B. (1894) *The Old Pike, A History of the National Road:* T. B. Searight, Pub., Uniontown, Pa.

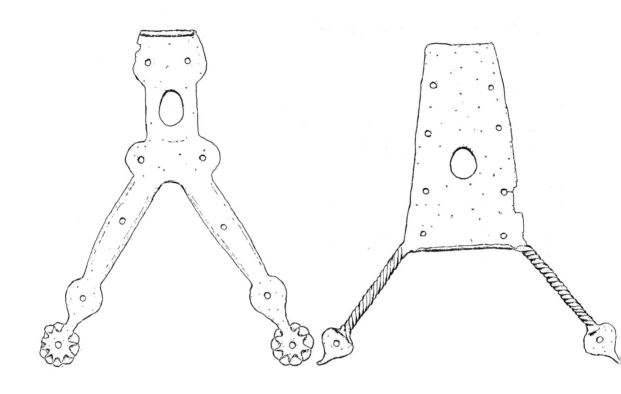

REAR HOUND PLATES

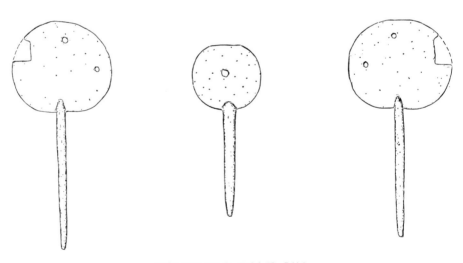

COUPLING POLE PIN
REAR HOUND PINS

154

Chapter 12

Nomenclature of Wagon Parts

A CONESTOGA wagon is a complicated structure of wood and iron containing many parts. In order to study and appreciate these wagons and to compare details from wagon to wagon a standard nomenclature for parts is almost a necessity. The Amos Gingrich wagon, presently on display at the Pennsylvania Farm Museum of Landis Valley (FIG. 5, 6, 7), is a medium sized vehicle of such excellent architecture and classic beauty that it can be regarded as the Conestoga wagon at its best. In 1925 Paul E. Garber of the U. S. National Museum took the necessary measurements, sketches, and photographs of this wagon so that detailed scale drawings of it could be made. Donald W. Holst prepared the scale drawings and these were published together with the names of the various parts in 1959 in a paper by Don H. Berkebile entitled "Conestoga Wagons in Braddock's Campaign 1755," U. S. National Museum Bulletin 218, pages 141-153. Through the courtesy of The Smithsonian Institution these drawings are reproduced here together with the names of the parts (FIG. 55, 56, 57).

FIGURE 55. (*opposite*) Scale drawings of the Gingrich wagon by Donald W. Holst, courtesy of The Smithsonian Institution.

BED AND RUNNING GEAR, RIGHT SIDE

1. Bows to support cloth cover.
2. Ridgepole or stringer.
3. Top rail, with bow staples and side-board staples.
4. Side-boards, removable.
5. Feedbox in traveling position.
6. Rubbing plates to prevent wheels from wearing wooden frame.
7. Side-board standards, forming framework of sides and projecting above top rail.
8. Standard, or upright, reinforcing side framing.
9. Securing rings for the ends of the spread chains, two of which span the bed to give extra support to the sides against inside pressures.
27. Upper front bolster, part of the wagon bed.
32. Bottom side rail.
53. Mid rail, or middle side rail.

REAR END GATE, AND FRONT END PANEL

1. Bow.
34. Staples for rear end gate standards.
35. End gate hasps and hooks.
36. Pins to secure gate to upper side rails.
37. Crossbar to give extra support to end gate.
38. Bottom end rail.
39. Middle end rail.
40. Top end rail.
41. Standard, or upright, forming end framing.
42. End boards.
43. Corner plates.

TONGUE, OR POLE, TOP AND SIDE VIEWS

10. Doubletree hasp, shown in proper position over the doubletree in the lower drawing; the hammer-headed doubletree pin goes through it, then through the doubletree and tongue.
11. Wear plates for doubletree pin.
12. Feedbox staple; in use, the feedbox sits on top of the tongue with the iron lug on one end stuck under this staple while the pin at the other end fits in the hole for the doubletree pin.
13. Hitching rings, for securing horses while feeding.
14. End ring, for securing spreader and fifth chain.

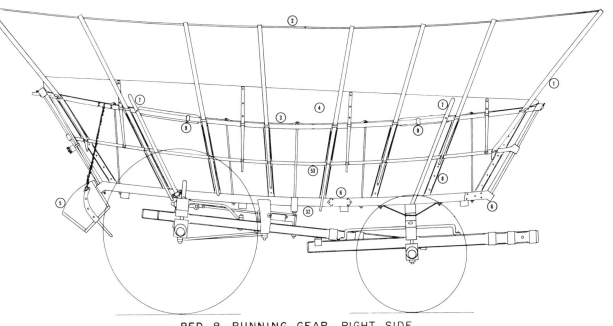

BED & RUNNING GEAR, RIGHT SIDE

0 1 2 3 4 5 6 FEET

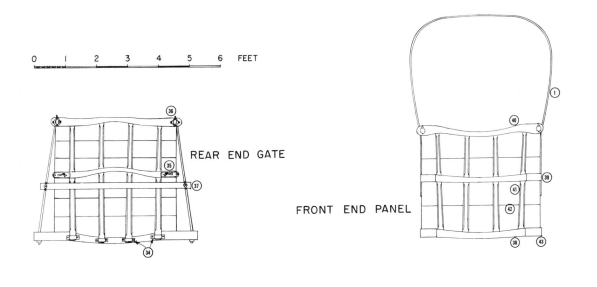

REAR END GATE

FRONT END PANEL

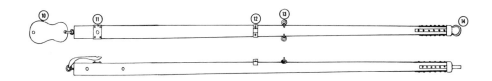

TONGUE OR POLE, TOP & SIDE VIEWS

157

FIGURE 56. Scale drawings of the Gingrich wagon, by Donald W. Holst, courtesy of The Smithsonian Institution.

RUNNING GEAR, TOP VIEW

15. Front hounds.
16. Rear hounds.
17. Lower front bolster, with axletree directly underneath.
18. Rear bolster, with axletree directly underneath.
19. Coupling pole.
20. Brake beam.
21. Brake beam shelf, or support.
49. Segments of iron forming the fifth wheel; these prevented the bed from toppling, or swaying excessively, on turns.
50. Rear brace for front hounds, to keep tongue from dropping.

FRONT AXLETREE AND BOLSTERS, FRONT VIEW

17. Lower front bolster, showing wear plates.
26. Front axletree with axle showing ironing.
27. Upper front bolster, part of the wagon bed.

REAR AXLETREE AND BOLSTER, REAR VIEW

18. Rear bolster.
28. Rear axletree, showing linchpin in position in right axle.
29. Hook and staple for holding tar pot.
30. Hound pin.

FRONT WHEEL AND REAR WHEEL

44. Wagon tire.
45. Hub, or nave.
46. Boxings, of cast iron, wedged in hub to take wear of axle.
47. Spoke.
48. Felly, or felloe.

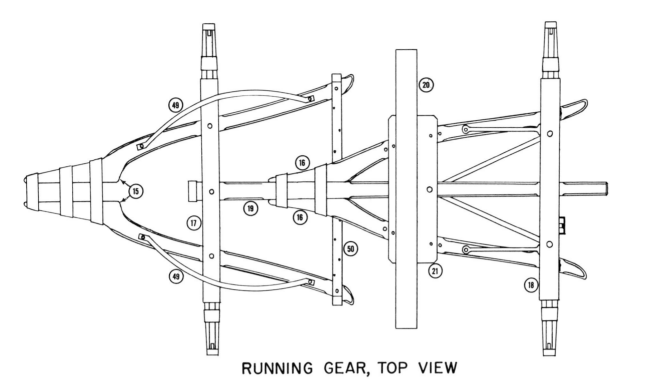

RUNNING GEAR, TOP VIEW

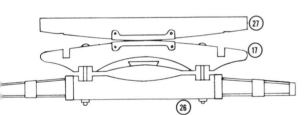

FRONT AXLETREE & BOLSTERS,
FRONT VIEW

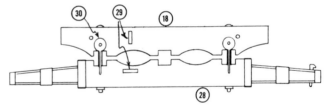

REAR AXLETREE & BOLSTER,
REAR VIEW

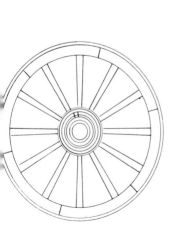

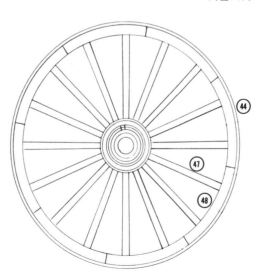

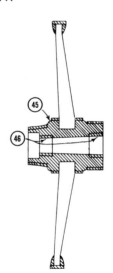

FRONT WHEEL

REAR WHEEL

FIGURE 57. Scale drawings of the Gingrich wagon, by Donald W. Holst, courtesy of The Smithsonian Institution.

FLOOR OF WAGON BOX, UNDERSIDE

18. Position of rear bolster when bed is on running gear.
27. Upper front bolster, showing hole for kingpin.
31. Cross beams, the center and rear ones being heavier, and projecting at the ends to hold the iron side braces.
32. Bottom side rails.
33. Floor boards.

FEEDBOX OR FEED TROUGH

5. Top, side, and end views; side view shows pin and lug for securing to tongue; end view shows bracket into which the chains hooked for traveling.

BRAKE MECHANISM DETAIL AND SECTION

16. Rear hound.
19. Coupling pole.
20. Brake beam.
21. Brake beam shelf, or support.
22. Brake rocker bar, with squared end for brake lever.
23. Rods connecting rocker bar to brake beam.
24. Brakeshoe, made of wood, but often faced with leather.
25. Brake lever, often 4 or 5 feet long.

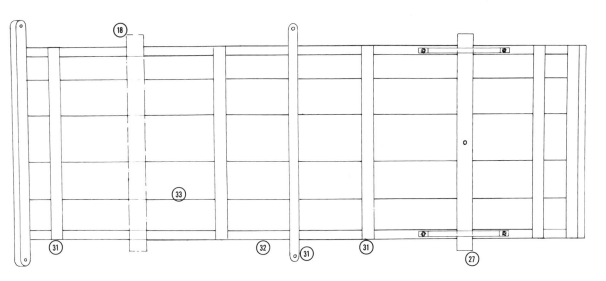

FLOOR OF WAGON, UNDERSIDE

0   1   2   3   4   5   6   FEET

TOOLBOX

FEEDBOX

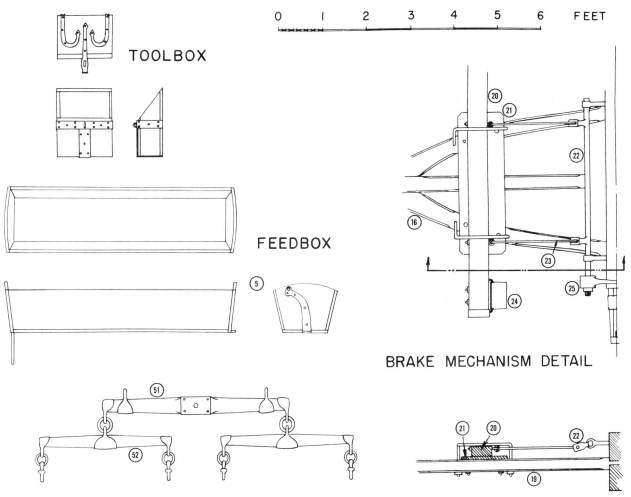

BRAKE MECHANISM DETAIL

DOUBLETREE, WITH SINGLETREES ATTACHED

BRAKE MECHANISM SECTION

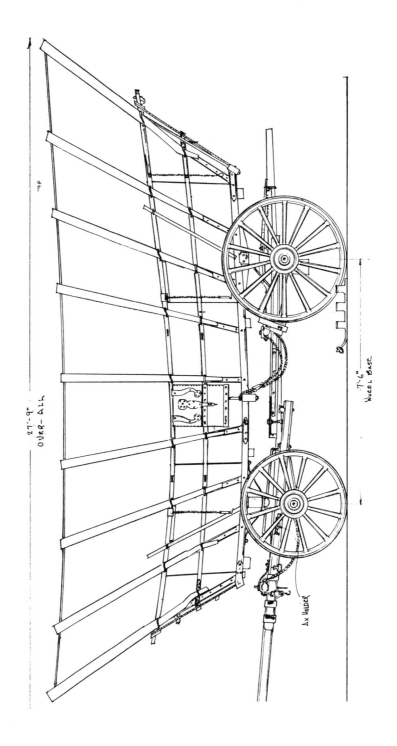

27'-9"
OVER-ALL

7'-6"
WHEEL BASE

Ax Holder

FIGURE 58. Scale drawing of a Conestoga wagon from Lancaster, now owned by Mr. & Mrs. James A. Keillor. A photograph of the same wagon is shown as FIG. 25.

Chapter 13

The Building of a Wagon

by William Henry Stanton

Excerpts from a book entitled *Our Ancestors, the Stantons:*
Philadelphia, 1922

WHO shall tell us about the wheelwright or wagon maker of those early days—that "white oak artist"—and his "wagon studio" decorated about the door with splotches of red lead, blue, green and yellow paint?

Often an unpretentious building, time had trimmed the inside in harmonious tones of brown and gray. Along the wall stood the bench with straight, solid, heavy, wood top; there was the wooden screw and lever, both polished smooth by long use, and such a heavy vise!

On the wall the racks for tools—and such a lot of them: planes, saws, chisels, bits of all sizes, draw knives, spoke shaves, gauges, squares and many more. All showed signs of long use, but were bright, well ground and sharp; it would have been less dangerous to strike the wagon maker's shild or kick his dog than to "nick" one of those tools. Farther along were wood patterns for hounds, fellies, bolsters, axles, spokes and the various parts of the wagon. Out on the floor was the chopping block, a section of a log set on end, with a hand-ax sticking in it—no one ever laid a hand-ax down! Farther toward the rear was the old round stove with cracks in the fire bowl and the crooked pipe that seemed ready to fall down.

Then there was the wagon maker himself—a man of medium height, all bone and muscle; dressed in gray, with gray beard and gray hair, too, but a clear, sharp eye nevertheless; and a soft felt hat, one time black, but now gray with dust, the right brim rolled up from many handlings, the band soaked many times with honest sweat; and such hands—horny palms and knotty knuckles, but no matter, they fitted the tool handles and that was all that was necessary.

He did not talk much unless you said "wagon", then the words just rolled along in endless procession. For the small boy he ran out his choice conundrum, "Over the hills and over the hills and always has its tongue out?" He went to church on Sunday because he wanted to do right, and he roused up when the minister mentioned "chariots and horses" or the "oaks of Bashan"; anyhow it helped to fill in the time until Monday morning when he could live his normal life and carve out those wooden works of art in his shop.

He knew wagons, could see one around the corner and tell who made it before it came in sight! He knew timber, too, thought God never made a better tree than the white oak and he would not have cared if He had not made any other. He picked out his timber "on the stump", chopped the tree down, cut off the logs, and had it sawed in great thick boards or slabs, then "stuck them up" in the yard on good foundation with sticks between and shaded from the sun so they could dry or "season" slowly and not crack. A year or two later they were brought into the shop for the finishing course in seasoning.

When the timber was ready for use a piece was carefully selected, and here the "cub" or apprentice was called in—that husky boy of undeveloped mind who was expected to have a well-developed back, a boy ready to work and anxious to learn. Here he was allowed to do a man's part and carry one end of the heavy plank to the stout trestles on the floor. Several layers of dust were swept off and the piece very carefully inspected. Then the patterns were laid down and placed to cut to the best advantage. Around each pattern the wagon maker cut a mark with a gouge scribe, which made a little round groove which he could see plainly.

The patterns were then laid aside, and now his interest began to grow, for though the plank was dark and unattractive he knew the beauty on the inside and was impatient to get it out. The rip-saw and meat rind came down and he began. Think of sawing by hand a dry, hard oak plank some three inches thick; but evidently he enjoyed the work and each time he moved his trusty saw he sent it just that much farther through the wood. Generally he chewed tobacco—if the wood was extra hard more was required. Soon that piece was out and turned over to the "cub" to chip off some parts with the hand-ax, and woe betide him if he cut "below the line."

Over on the bench, the side from which to lay out the work was planed down straight and out of "wind"—no need for a straight-edge or square, he had them both in his clear eye, and when he held the piece up to get the proper light and took a "squint" at it even his critical exactness could find no need for a tool.

Then the piece was carefully and accurately "laid off" and other sides were worked down; much of the work was done with "draw" knives of various sizes. As a surface was finished what beautiful "grain" was exposed, and such delicate tints—it was genuine white oak, not red oak, nor chestnut, nor Spanish oak, nor any other one of the two dozen varieties that now pass for "oak", neither was it "dead" and worm eaten—worms do not live in "live" timber! It was tough, very tough, and hard and had the peculiar stain gloss that indicates great strength and long life.

How the wagon maker enjoyed his chosen task! He knew the timber was reliable and he put into the work the best skill he possessed. He rounded out the most beautiful curves, circles and ovals and tangents to them—every cut he made seemed so easy, the piece just changed shape as a flower develops in a moving picture. How he enjoyed his work! It was all good, honest labor. The "fits" were all fits —"glue joints" that would "pinch a hair." What did he care for "more wages, shorter hours, and better working condition", work was pleasure and the consciousness of work well done was good pay.

So one piece after another was carved out. Now a new pleasure— to fit those pieces together to make the whole complete. The wheel was given the proper "dish"—an arch effect, the tire was the "shew back" and the hub the "keystone," thus giving greater strength to the wheel to carry the greater strain when on the low side of the road; the axles were tapered so that the spokes would stand vertically from the hub down and carry the load and all the angle given from the hub upward; also the wheels were given sufficient "lead" to prevent the hubs from running hard against either the collar or the linch pin.

When all was complete, the wagon maker with many fears trusted his treasure to the blacksmith to be "ironed." There was a perennial quarrel on between the two—the ironwork was not so good as the woodwork, and the woodwork was not so good as the ironwork, but any impartial judge would have admired both. The iron in the hands of the blacksmith seemed to turn just the way he wanted it to, of to flatten out and round itself off at the corner; he did not "beat" it into shape, but just tapped a little here and there and trimmed it off a little, patted it "easy like" with his hammer and behold the pieces were fitted for the woodwork, in size and curve nicely matching the parts of the wood. The tires were bent and welded after careful trials with his "traveler" wheel to get them just the right size, not too loose nor yet too tight, as this would injure the fellies. They were then heated in a circular wood-fire in the yard and when just hot enough were slipped on the wheel and quickly cooled—to burn the fellies was the "unpardonable sin" in the mind of the wagon maker. There was indeed a friendly rivalry as to who should do the best work, and make a heavy edition of that famous one-horse shay, every piece of which you remember was made equally good and strong so that no one part gave out before the other.

At last the wagon was finished; then came the painting—the best of linseed oil and "red lead" for the running gears, with the body finished in green or blue and the name, maybe, Isaac Perry, or Uriah Bailey, plainly painted on the side. Every effort was made to make the best; neither labor nor material was spared to secure this result. And when one day some farmer drove away from the shop with "the best wagon ever made" the artist heaved a sigh and felt as if he had parted forever from his long-time friend, but he wisely hid his sorrow, and—began carving out another masterpiece.

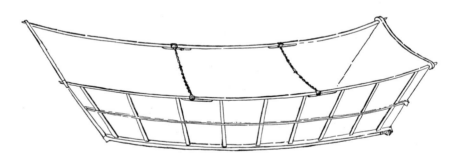

TOP RAIL SPREAD CHAINS

Chapter 14
Wagon Beds or Boxes

THE box or bed of a Conestoga wagon is considerably more complex in structure than the simple rectangular boxes used on wagons in the late nineteenth century, and of course there were sound reasons for this complexity. Early roads were incredibly rough at times and only a flexible, yielding structure could stand up long to the torture of travel under heavy load. There were no springs between the box and the axles upon which it rested, yet a certain amount of yield someplace in the system was absolutely necessary if burdens of a number of thousand pounds were to be hauled for days on end over these roads. It was not a box that was needed, but a gigantic basket. The Conestoga wagon was, in fact, this basket on a set of wheels. Well-built boats and ships, too, are designed and built to yield to the unending and varied stresses of the waves. A particularly good type of boat to consider as the sea-going analog of a Conestoga wagon is the lapstrake boat of Scandanavia, whose sides are constructed of relatively thin boards fastened together with copper rivets. Such boats are light in weight for their size, they "give" under the stresses of load and wave, and they last a long, long time.

The Conestoga bed makes contact with the running gear that supports it at only three points, two at the stern and one at the forward end. The rear portion of the bed rests firmly on the rear bolster, contact being made by the lower side rails which usually are armored underneath with a heavy iron strap in the region of contact. The upper front bolster (FIG. 56), which is attached to the wagon bed permanently, has a sturdy iron rub plate at its center and has a lower surface that slopes upward away from this rub plate. The upper surface of the lower front bolster is convex upward. The upper front bolster, and consequently the whole front end of the wagon box, can rock back and forth though held in place by the king pin. This also makes it possible for either one of the front wheels to ride over a rock or to drop into a hole without damaging the wagon or disturbing the contents too much. And if the obstacle calls for more displacement than the upper and lower bolsters allow, the front end of the wagon bed can yield even though the rear portion keeps on an even keel. So flexible is the Conestoga box that a relatively small pressure from the hand will suffice to move one side of it up or down if applied at the front end.

The floor of a Conestoga box had a characteristic curvature to it, being lowest near the center and sloping upward at the ends. The standard explanation for this is that it was made this way purposely to keep the load centered. This seems like a reasonable answer until it is brought to mind that the days of the Conestoga were over by mid-century and that in the latter half of the nineteenth century and first two decades of the twentieth century thousands and thousands of freight and farm wagons were made and used and almost all of these had flat-bottomed rectangular-sided boxes of simple construction.

Another possible reason for the curvature of the box is appearance. The wagon was developed at a time, and in a place, when and where those who used them cared enough for beauty to demand it and to pay for it. A wagon with a high bow and stern, and raked ends, has an appeal to the eye that no straight-sided wagon can match. Some wagon owners went to considerable pains to trim carefully the sail for optimum appearance. The original bows on the Gingrich wagon (FIG. 5, 6, 7), the wagon of J. A. Keillor (FIG. 25), and one wagon at the Henry Ford Museum (FIG. 24) have been purposely bent so that their tops are somewhat flattened, and the height of the tops of the bows above the floor of the wagon has been carefully adjusted so that the ridge of the bows has a curved line that conforms, more or less, with the curvature of the sides. There can be no doubt at all that the top rail of the front end panel is down-bowed merely for the sake of appearance, and likewise, that the top rail of the rear end gate is bowed up for the same reason. And some wagons, presumably later ones, are made with a floor and bottom rails that have little or no curvature, yet there is marked curvature to the top rail. It is difficult to find a functional use for a curved top rail on a wagon with a flat floor. And after all, vast sums are spent in the mid-twentieth century for automobile styling, to produce such things as functionally-useless bumpers of chrome, and tail fins.

But in spite of the argument that late nineteenth century wagons had flat bottoms there is reason to favor the argument that the concavity of the bed minimized load shifting. The chief function of the fully developed Conestoga in the sixty years following the Revolution was in carrying freight across the Appalachian mountains. The roads that wound their way up and down the mountains had continuous grades for many miles. Load shifting on the relatively short hills of the piedmont might have been a relatively minor problem, but on a long mountain grade the gradual shifting of a load of two or three or four tons could have been serious.

But this explanation does not account for the fact that medium and small sized wagons of basic Conestoga build, with distinctively curved sides, were made and used for farming purposes in the middle and late nineteenth century in Lancaster, York, and neighboring counties. Some of these wagons did not even carry bows, and obviously were not intended for long distance freighting. Old traditions die hard in southern Pennsylvania, and after a century of the manufacture and use of Conestogas it is probable that the tried and proven form was not discarded immediately, even though the simpler form would have done the job equally well, and at less cost.

A few decades ago some U. S. history books contained the explanation that the boat-like shape of the Conestoga wagon box was purposely made so that pioneers could float themselves and their goods across rivers that they had to cross. This is utter nonsense, for the box would leak like a sieve if placed in water.

The two curved side panels are the basic units from which the wagon box is built. Each panel contains the upper, middle, and lower side rails, the uprights, and the wide, thin boards that fill in the spaces between the rails and the uprights. The three rails are mortised so that the uprights pass through them, and generally the joints are not pinned. Frequently there are four iron tie rods of about 5/16 inch diameter that bind the upper and lower rails together. The boards that fill the spaces between the rails usually are not over 5/8 inch thick. They are fastened to the uprights on the inner side by a series of iron rivets. An iron strap about 1 inch wide and 1/16 to 3/32 inch thick runs parallel to each upright on the inner side of the boards, and the rivets fasten into this strap.

The front end panel, and the rear end gate are similarly constructed. Usually there are four uprights which are mortised through the upper, middle, and lower rails. The rear end gate, however, is removable and does not have a lower rail. The front end panel is a unit which is fastened to the front end of the side panels by mortised joints. In this case the side rails project forward and pass into mortises in the three rails of the front panel. Iron straps pass around the corners of the middle and lower rails at the front end to hold the front panel firmly in place. The top side rails, however, pass through holes in the upper rail of the front panel and project a few inches beyond, and pins of iron are put through the projecting top rails to hold the pieces firmly in place.

The side panels are connected by four transverse beams of oak approximately 2 by 2 1/2 inches in section. The ends of these beams are held to the under side of the side rails by heavy iron staples—roughly equivalent to "U" bolts. The front bolster is an additional transverse tie, which is held in place by bolts through the lower side rails and by iron straps. In the center of the box is still another transverse beam. This projects 6 to 8 inches beyond the outer side of the side rails and carries the heavy iron brace rods which hold the sides in an upright position.

The oaken floor boards are 1/2 to 3/4 inch thick and run lengthwise of the wagon. Usually an odd number of boards is used, 3 or 5, perhaps so that the king pin hole will be in the center of a board instead of at the joint between two boards.

Conestoga wagon boxes can be classified arbitrarily as large, medium or small on the basis a length measurement. To form a basis for comparison of wagon sizes, the inside dimensions of a number of boxes were taken (TABLE). Construction details differ from wagon to wagon making outside dimensions less desirable than those inside where the pay load was kept. The width of the wagon, inside across the floor, usually is about 42 inches. This standardized dimension results from the fact that the distance between the two wheels on a given axle was standardized so that tire centers were about 60 inches apart. The length of the box, inside, was essentially the length of the floor boards, but because of the considerable curvature to most beds, measurements of the chord rather than the arc were taken.

The measurements of length range from 13 feet 10 inches to 10 feet 5 inches. Larger boxes exceed 13 feet in length, and for purposes of discussion it is convenient to use 13 feet as an arbitrary lower limit for wagons termed "large." Only one really small wagon has been measured in this study, the Flowers wagon at Oglebay Park, Wheeling, which has a length of 10 feet 5 inches. The remainder of the wagons that have been measured range in length from 11 feet 8 inches to 12 feet, 9.5 inches, and it probably is best to consider all of these as

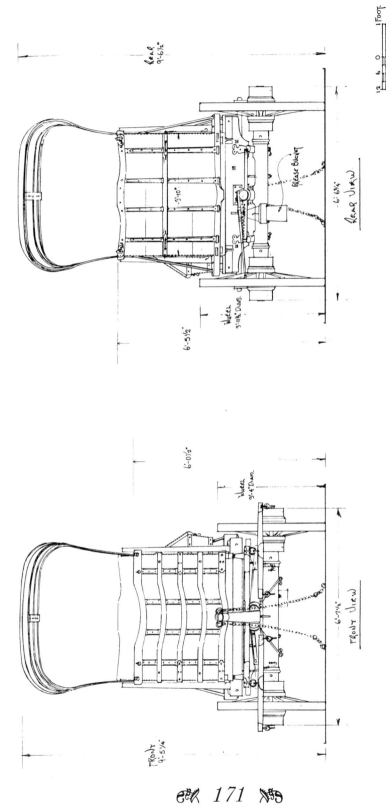

FIGURE 59. Scale drawings of a Conestoga wagon owned by Mr. & Mrs. James A. Keillor.

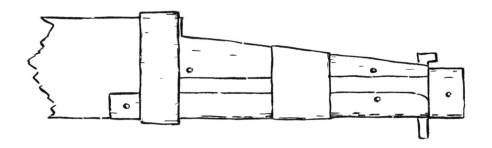

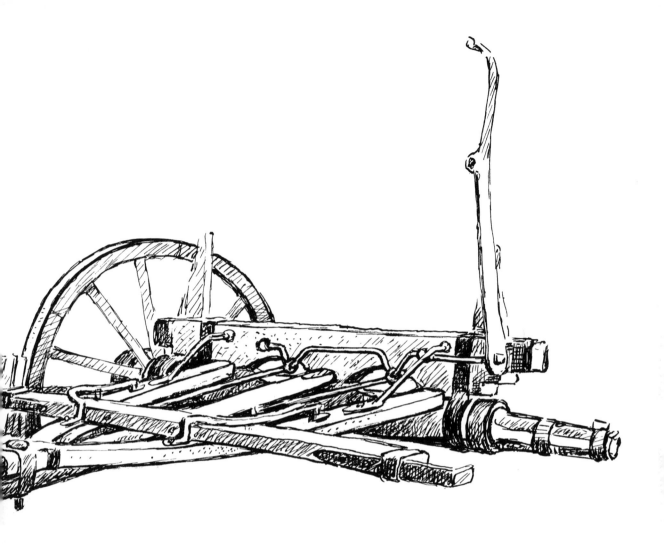

FIGURE 60. (left) Front section of a Conestoga wagon running gear. The axles are sheathed top and bottom with iron, and bound with three bands of iron, as shown in the detail drawing.

FIGURE 61. (above) Rear section of a Conestoga wagon running gear, with coupling pole attached.

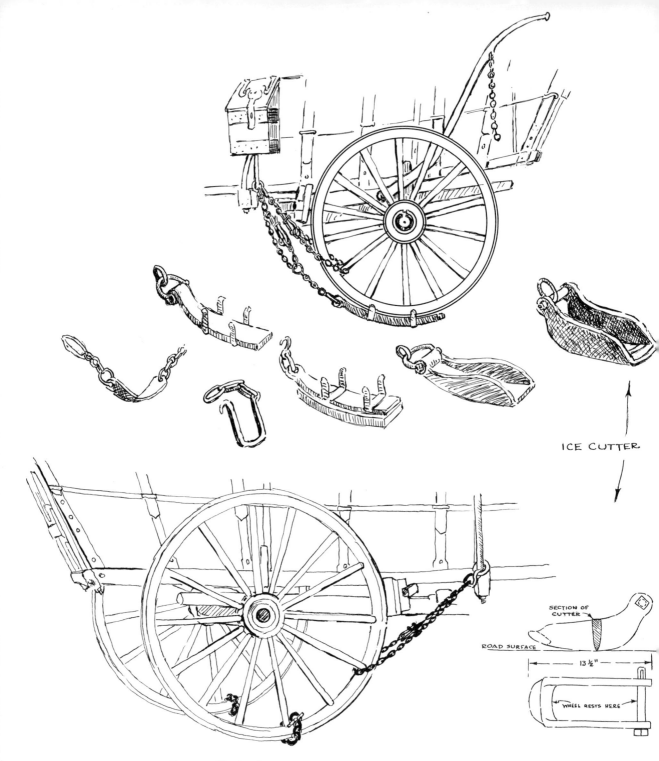

ICE CUTTER

SECTION OF
CUTTER

ROAD SURFACE

13½"

WHEEL RESTS HERE

FIGURE 62. On long steep inclines a heavily-laden wagon could not be held back with the brake mechanism. Then the rear wheels were chained to the wagon box and the wagon was skidded down the hill. To prevent wear on the tires various drag shoes were used, and for extra retardation short chains, known as rough locks, were fastened around each tire and felly at the point of contact with the road. A special ice cutter prevented side slipping.

174

medium sized and to set a lower limit for this category at 11 feet 6 inches.

The number of bows that a wagon carried was related to the length of the bed, although the correspondence is not exact. The minimum number of bows is 8 and the maximum number is 13 (Burgner wagon, FIG. 28). Wagons in the large category carry 10 or more bows, and those of medium size have 8 or 9. It is entirely possible, however, that an 8 or 9 bow box may exist that exceeds 13 feet in length.

Compared with the later farm wagons, the boxes of Conestogas are relatively deep. The height of the box, from the top of the floor to the top of the upper rail, measured at mid-section, in the vicinity of the tool box, exceeds 28 inches on all of the medium and large wagons, and in most cases exceeds 30 inches. This measurement exceeds 30 inches on all of the large wagons studied.

A tool box is almost invariably present on the left side of the wagon bed. This is a simple wooden box bound with iron and having a sloping wooden lid. The side of the wagon forms the back of the tool box. The most notable thing about tool boxes is that they often contain ornate iron hinges and lock hasps (FIG. 64, 65), and because of this have been sought after by antique dealers and collectors. If the blacksmith who ironed the wagon had any artistic inclinations, the tool box was the place for him to go all out. Pennsylvania Dutch tulip and bird head motifs frequently were used, but a variety of other designs less easily described also can be found on surviving tool boxes. It is probable that many of the wagons with Pennsylvania Dutch motifs on the tool box lids were made in the Pennsylvania Dutch region of southern Pennsylvania, but inasmuch as these designs were both simple and appealing they could have been used also by makers in Maryland, Virginia, and Ohio. It is sad but true that many a fine Conestoga wagon has had its side cut in two with a saw in order that the tool box could be taken from it, after which the remains of the wagon were consigned to the fire or left to rot.

Most Conestoga wagon beds were equipped with side boards which could be added above the top rail to increase the carrying capacity. The tops of these side boards were almost always straight while the lower edge was curved to conform to the curvature of the top rail. Traditionally they were painted red, in contrast to the light blue color that was used on the outside of the wagon box. They were held in place by uprights that fit into staples in the side of the wagon bed.

Most wagon boxes have special side board standards that were mortised into the front bolster where it extended beyond the lower side rail, and extend up along the outside of the middle and upper side rails to project a few inches above the top of the upper rail.

Ornate ironwork sometimes is found in other places on a Conestoga bed besides the tool box. Reinforcing plates of iron are used at the corners of the structure, and on some wagons the ends of these plates are made into decorative finials. Likewise, the rubbing plates on the lower rail that protected it from wear by the front wheel sometimes are decoratively terminated on either end. Often the foremost and hindmost bow staples on the upper side rail are S-shaped rather than straight, and of course this was merely for decoration.

A number of chains are attached to the wagon bed at various places for very specific reasons. Chains for supporting the feed trough are attached to the upper side rails near the rear end. One, and sometimes two, short chains are secured to the upper top rail in the central part of the box. When the wagon was heavily loaded these were fastened to the top rail on the opposite side to prevent the sides from spreading. Heavy chains are attached to the middle iron side braces for the purpose of locking the rear wheels as a means of braking the wagon when descending long hills.

The sloping rear end gate sometimes requires extra support against the pressures of loads, and this is provided by a horizontal bar of oak fastened to the rear brace rods by means of wing nuts. Some blacksmith-artists even took time to add art to lowly wing nuts (FIG. 73).

The traditional color for the Conestoga wagon bed was blue, but there is no particular shade and hue that can be considered as the one and only authentic one. The original paint on surviving wagons ranges from a light blue-grey to a light blue-green, although paint with a greenish tint is less common. Paint was used sparingly on the beds. Almost always the entire inside of the bed as well as the inside of the tool box and the bottom of the bed were unpainted.

The cloth covers for Conestoga wagons were made either of homespun hemp, or of cotton sailcloth or canvas. A great deal of homespun linen was produced in southeastern Pennsylvania in the eighteenth century and it was natural that a farmer would use his home made product in preference to laying out cash for cloth made in a factory. Canvas and sailcloth undoubtedly were available in Philadelphia from the earliest times inasmuch as they were produced in abundance in England and widely used in the shipping industry. In 1718 James Logan bought twenty yards of Luback canvas for his wagon.

The appearance of a Conestoga wagon is affected considerably by the care used in arranging the bows and in tailoring the cloth cover. The profile of the ridge pole, the height of the bows above the top rail, and the shape of the bows must be considered with care, for each wagon bed has its own characteristics. It should be noted that the profile of the ridge pole of the Gingrich wagon (FIG. 55) has a greater radius of curvature (i.e. is flatter) than the curved profile of the top rail. The curved line of the top rail is important to the appearance of the wagon, hence the rail should not be obscured by a cloth cover that extends down beyond it and which perhaps does not conform to the same curve.

Table of CONESTOGA WAGON BOX AND WHEEL DIMENSIONS

Wheel dimensions in parentheses are for running gears probably not original to the beds.
Dimensions in inches except for box length

Wagon name, owner and location	Number of bows	Box length inside	Box width inside	Box height inside	Rear wheel dia.	Front wheel dia.	Tire width Rear	Front
Greist wagon York Hist. Soc. York, Pa.	12	13′ 10″	42	33	(58)	(44)	(3.75)	(3.5)
(unnamed) Franklin & Marshall Coll., Lancaster, Pa.	12	13′ 6″	41.5	31	60	48	3	3
(unnamed) Oglebay Park Wheeling, W. Va.	11	13′ 5.5″	42	32	(52)	(35)	(4)	(4)
(unnamed) Penna. Farm Museum Landis Valley, Pa.	11	13′ 5″	41.75	30.5	65	48	3.75	3.75
(unnamed) Hagley Museum Wilmington, Del.	12	13′ 4″	41	32	68.5	50	3.75	3.75
(unnamed) Bruce Myers Quarryville, Pa.	12	13′ 0″	42	30.5	(60)	(43)	(4)	(4)

Wagon name, owner and location	Number of bows	Box length inside	Box width inside	Box height inside	Rear wheel dia.	Front wheel dia.	Tire width	
							Rear	Front
(unnamed) Smithsonian Inst. Washington, D. C.	11	13' 0"	42	32	68.5	48	4	4
Christian Herr Penna. Farm Museum Landis Valley, Pa.	10	13' 0"	45	30.5	55.5	40	3.75	4
Quickel wagon George Shumway York, Pa.	9	12' 9.5"	42	31.5	—	—		
Gingrich wagon Penna. Farm Museum Landis Valley, Pa.	8	12' 6"	43	28.5	60	44	3.5	3.5
(unnamed) Henry Ford Museum Dearborn, Mich.	8	12' 4"	41.25	26	65	50	4	4
(unnamed) Bruce Myers Quarryville, Pa.	9	11' 11"	42	29	—	—		
(unnamed) Penna. Farm Museum Landis Valley, Pa.	8	11' 11"	41.5	28	(54)	(43)	(3)	(3)
(unnamed) Penna. Farm Museum Landis Valley, Pa.	8	11' 8"	41.5	29	60	48	3	3
(unnamed) R. Dietrich Pittsburgh, Pa.	8	11' 8"	43	31.5	—	—		
Flowers wagon Oglebay Park Wheeling, W. Va.	8	10' 5"	40.5	21.5	40.5	33	3.5	3.5

Note: Painted on the tail gate is the information that this was made by W. Musselman in 1836 at Somerset, Ohio.

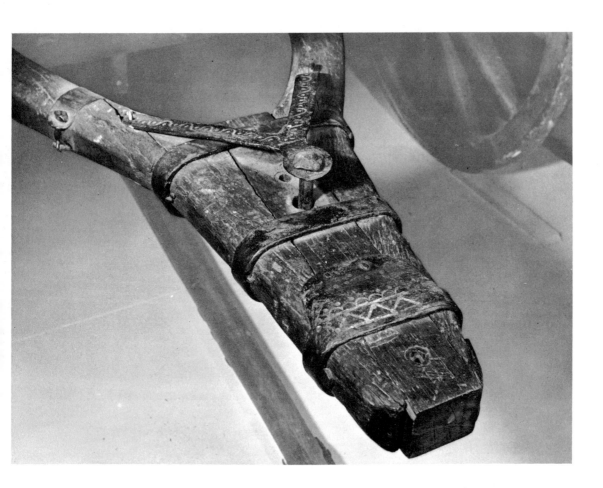

FIGURE 63. (above) Front hound bands and doubletree hasp of the Weber wagon. *Ontario Dept. Travel & Publicity, Toronto, Ontario.* (below) A doubletree hasp decorated with a blacksmith's initials and the date 1851. *Mr. & Mrs. James A. Keillor.*

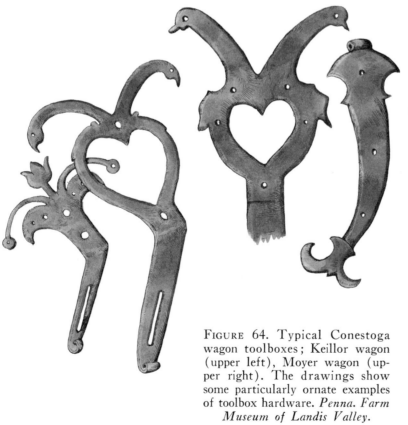
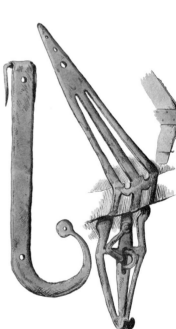

FIGURE 64. Typical Conestoga wagon toolboxes; Keillor wagon (upper left), Moyer wagon (upper right). The drawings show some particularly ornate examples of toolbox hardware. *Penna. Farm Museum of Landis Valley.*

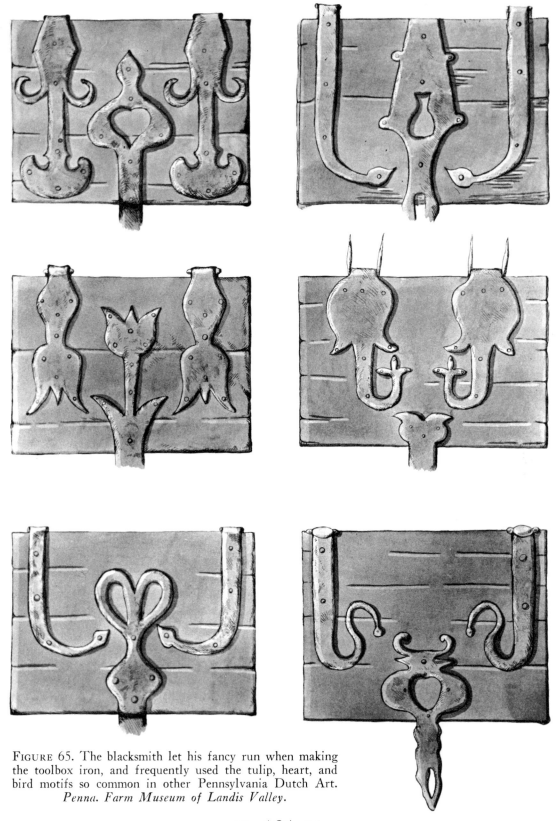

FIGURE 65. The blacksmith let his fancy run when making the toolbox iron, and frequently used the tulip, heart, and bird motifs so common in other Pennsylvania Dutch Art. *Penna. Farm Museum of Landis Valley.*

181

Figure 66. Contents of a toolbox. A traveling wagoner probably would keep in his box a few particularly useful tools and a number of extra small parts, such as some of these: (*left to right*) all-purpose pinchers; corncobs to use in wheel hubs to keep kinch pins from bouncing out; eel skin for harness repairs; open links; nuts and wing nuts; single tree and doubletree hardware; tar pot hook; snaps and cockeyes; jaw-breaker bit and ordinary bit; harness buckles; padlock for toolbox; nails and bolts; horseshoes; assorted staples; linch pin; horseshoe nails; rasp for horse hoof trimming; washers; Little Brown Jug and gimlet, used by wagoners to steal their supply of whiskey from the barrels they hauled — a barrel hoop was driven up, a hole bored with the gimlet, the jug was filled, and the hole was plugged and the hoop replaced; hammer; horse chestnut to keep away rheumatism.

Chapter 15

Running Gear

THE standard Conestoga wagon running gear features wooden axles sheathed top and bottom with iron clouts, and wheels that are kept in place by iron linch pins (FIG. 60, 61). The four-wheeled gear is made up of two separate assemblies; the rear portion contains the rear axletree, rear hounds, bolster, rear wheels, and the coupling pole; the front portion contains the front axletree, front hounds, the front bolster, front wheels, and tongue. The front and rear portions are of similar construction, although they differ in details. Basically, each portion consists of a triangular frame with two wheels attached and with a long pole attached to the forward apex. The rear brake mechanism can be thought of as a useful but not absolutely necessary part of the running gear. Some Conestogas did not have any mechanical brake.

The front hounds are the sturdy oak pieces that form the connection between the tongue and the front axletree. Where they join the axletree they are sandwiched between the axletree and the lower front bolster and pinned in place by a long bolt running through all three pieces. The triangular construction cannot be surpassed for rigidity and simplicity. The hounds serve other purposes also. They extend behind the front axle and at their after end are tied together by a transverse brace of oak armored on the top with a strap of iron. This brace keeps the long and heavy tongue from falling to the ground because the coupling pole passes over it. The hounds also serve to support the curved pieces of iron known as the "fifth wheel." These prevent the front portion of the wagon bed from swaying excessively or toppling on turns.

The left front hound holds the iron sheath in which the trusty axe was kept. This feature is almost invariably found on the running gear of a Conestoga wagon and can rightly be regarded as a small but important detail. The axe sheath also was a place where blacksmith artistry came to light at times (FIG. 67). Fish designs of iron were used as well as others that are fanciful but do not necessarily represent something. A simple ring shaped somewhat like a figure eight and fastened to the tongue by means of a staple holds the handle of the axe. The axe obviously was important to the Conestoga wagoner, and it was particularly important in the earlier days when the roads cut through miles of woodland. Trees might fall across the trail to block the way for the wagon, or a pole would be needed to bend against the rear wheel for a brake in descending a hill, or a heavy log would be needed to drag behind the wagon for the same purpose, or firewood might be needed for an evening campfire. Furthermore, the handy axe could be used for emergency repairs such as making a tongue or even an axletree.

The tongue is secured to the front hounds by means of a single transverse pin of iron, but two or three bands of iron are used to bind the three parts securely together. These bands are driven onto the wedge-shaped front ends of the hounds and retained by friction alone. Frequently these front hound bands were decorated by the blacksmiths who made them, and occasionally a name or a date is present on them. Typical hound band decorations are found on the Weber wagon, which pre-dates 1807 (FIG. 21).

The tongue or pole is a straight piece of oak about twelve feet long. At its forward end is a large ring of iron into which the spreader is hooked. The middle pair of horses of the six-horse team pull against this spreader. The long fifth chain which transmits the pull of the lead horses sometimes also is fastened into this end ring and sometimes it connects to a separate ring located about eighteen inches from the end of the pole, and underneath. Near the middle of the pole there may be one or more hitching rings to secure the horses while feeding. Near the middle of the pole there also is an iron staple or piece of strap iron made to take the lug at the forward end of the feedbox when it is placed on top of the tongue. At the after end of the pole, in the region of the hounds is a hole into which fits the doubletree pin. This hole also takes the pin on the after end of the feedbox, to hold the box in place securely. Usually an iron hasp is attached at the rear end of the pole also, to provide better support for the pull of the doubletree. Sometimes these doubletree hasps were decorated by the blacksmiths, and in one case a date was placed upon one (FIG. 63).

The method of attaching the tongue to the front hounds was standard, but two different methods were used for joining the rear hounds to the coupling pole. The coupling pole must be regarded as the least permanent part of the running gear. Its purpose is to join the rear portion of the gear to the front portion, and to make it possible to adjust the distance between the front and rear axletrees. Some gears have the front ends of the rear hounds joined together tightly so that the coupling pole passes underneath them, and on others the coupling pole passes between the hounds (FIG. 56).

Probably the earliest method was for the hounds to be directly joined so that the pole ran below them. A Y-shaped plate of iron was fastened across the top of the two hounds, to help bind them together, and to provide extra support for the coupling pin which passed through a hole in this iron plate. These rear hound plates sometimes were ornately made, in spite of the fact that one would have to crawl under wagons to see them. Hounds of this type are secured to the coupling pole by means of a large iron pin, and by a band of iron that went around the front of the hounds and the coupling pole. The distance between the front and rear axletrees is adjusted easily by placing holes in the pole wherever needed. If the occasion arose that the running gear was needed to haul something of great length, such as long poles or some bulky structure, an extra long coupling pole could be made easily to suit the situation.

The after end of the coupling pole passes through a hole between the rear axletree and the rear bolster, and usually extends a foot or two behind where it makes a convenient place to hang a water bucket. It is necessary for the pole to pass through this hole because the hounds are connected to the pole only by the coupling pin.

The Conestoga wagon brake mechanism is a simple mechanical device operated by means of a long iron lever on the left side of the wagon and situated near the rear bolster. By means of this lever a rocker bar is turned, and this pulls the transverse brake beam to the rear so that the brake shoes which are mounted on the beam will make contact with the rear tires (FIG. 57). This side-operated brake is a classic feature of the later Conestoga wagon. An alternate type of brake lever, operated from the rear of the wagon, came into use in the middle of the nineteenth century, and often running gears of this period, and the late part of the century also, contained a rocker bar that could be operated by the rear lever or from a side lever that was easily added if desired. A number of the surviving Conestoga wagons presently are resting on running gear which once were equipped for the rear brake lever, either because these gears were made in the later period and originally were equipped with the rear brake, or because the rear brake levers were installed later on gears that had only the standard side brake at the start.

The mechanical brake probably did not appear on Conestoga wagons until early in the nineteenth century, when it was known as a "rubber." Before then, wagoners relied on less refined methods. Searight quotes the remarks of John Deets, an old wagoner who began driving in 1822, concerning the problem of braking on a hill:[1] ". . . but the trouble was in getting down, for they had no rubbers [brakes] then, and to tight lock would soon wear out the tires. They would cut a small pole about 10 or 11 feet long and tie it to the bed with the lock chain and then bend it against the hind wheel and tie it to the feed trough, or the hind part of the wagon bed, just tight enough to let the wheel turn slow. Sometimes one driver would wear out from 15 to 20 poles between Baltimore and Wheeling. Sometimes others would cut down a big tree and tie it to the hind end of the wagon and drop it at the foot of the hill." This suggests that the mechanical brake may not have appeared until after the first quarter of the century.

The standard Conestoga axle is a cone-shaped wooden extention of the oak axletree (FIG. 56, 61) which is shod on the top and bottom with pieces of iron called clouts. Three bands of iron hold the clouts in place. Near the end of the axle is a vertical hole which takes the linch pin that holds the wheel on the axle. Generally the front and rear axles are of the same size so that the wheels can be interchanged. The bottom of the cone-shaped axle necessarily has to be horizontal so that there will be no tendency for the wheel to move outward and push against the linch pin. However, a wheel on a cone-shaped axle, when moving over an irregular and sometimes soft roadbed, does not apply its force against the lowest part of the axle, but along an element of the cone slightly ahead of the lowest element. If a correcting measure is not taken, the wheel will move toward the outside and push against the linch pin. The correction is to give the axles a slight lead so that the wheels have a small toe-in.

At sometime near the middle of the nineteenth century the thimble skein axle came into use, but by then the days of the Conestoga were over. A conical skein of iron fitted entirely around the wooden axle and extended under the axletree where it was securely bolted. This provided a stronger axle than the standard Conestoga type. Some of these thimble skein axles were equipped with linch pins and some with a threaded nut to retain the wheel.

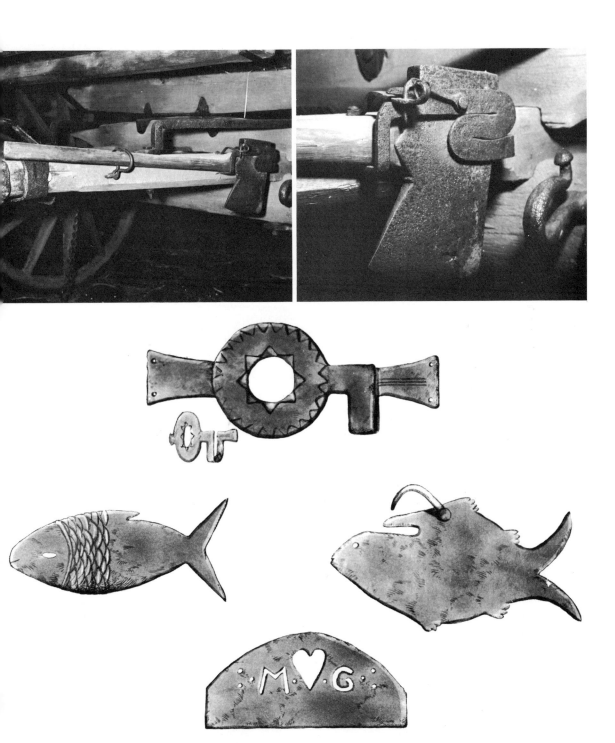

FIGURE 67. (above) An axe customarily was carried in a special iron sheath on the left front hound. These photographs show the axe in position on the Gingrich wagon. (below) Axe sheaths often were decorative as well as functional, as can be seen in these four drawings. *Penna Farm Museum of Landis Valley.*

FIGURE 68. The tar pot carried pine tar for lubricating the axles. Usually it was turned from a poplar log and made in the standard shape shown by these typical examples. A wooden bucket for watering horses was part of the wagon equipment also. *Tar pot photos by Einars J. Mengis, courtesy Shelburne Museum, Inc.*

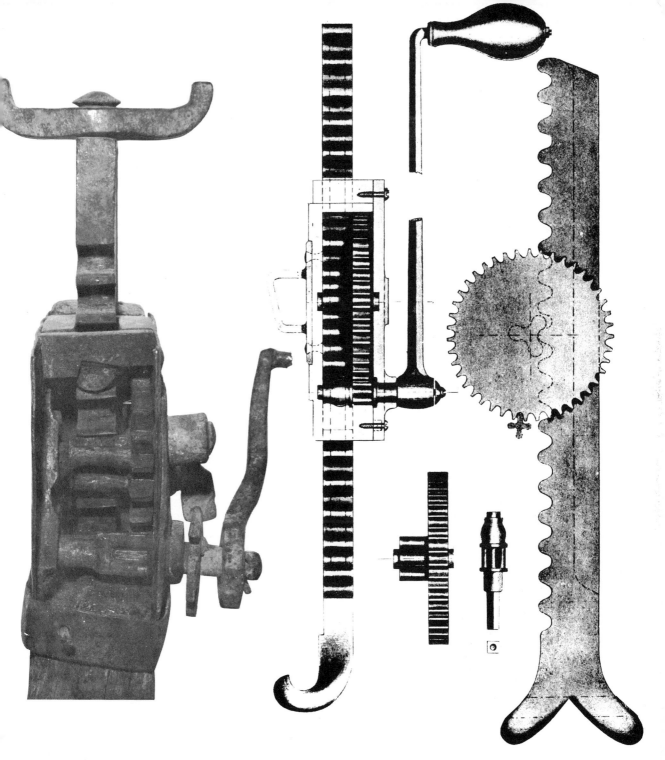

FIGURE 69. The mechanism of a Conestoga wagon jack is nearly identical to that of a European crossbow cranequin. In each case the handle turns a four-toothed pinion, but whereas the large gear of the cranequin has 43 teeth, the jack's large gear has about 18 teeth. In each case the rack is moved by means of a three-toothed pinion. The mechanical advantage of jacks varies from piece to piece, but lies between 50 and 80. *Cranequin drawing from "The Crossbow" by Sir Ralph Payne-Gallwey, The Holland Press, London, 1958.*

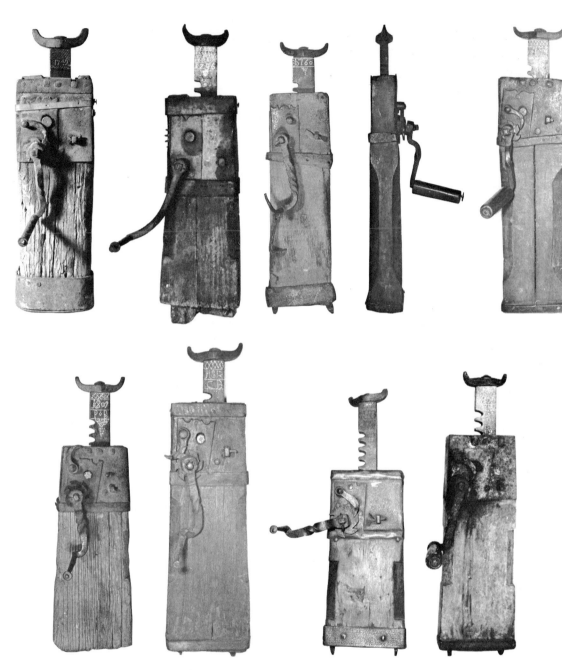

FIGURE 70. (above) Wagon jacks of 1749, 1756, 1760, 1794 (front and side) ; (below) jacks of 1809, 1813, 1818, 1855. Note that the jacks of 1756 and 1760 are not equipped with a ratchet wheel and pawl. *Photos, and ownership: 1749, Ohio Historical Soc., Columbus, O.; 1756 & 1855, W. S. Redhed, Homer, Ill.; 1760 & 1809, Shelburne Museum, Shelburne, Vt.; 1794 & 1813, G. Shumway; 1818, J. A. Keillor.*

Conestoga wheels were made in a range of sizes to suit the service intended and the size of the wagon. The largest wheels were used on the heavy trans-mountain freighters, or Pitt wagons of the 1820-1850 period. Generally the rear wheels on these big wagons had a diameter between 60 inches and 70 inches (TABLE), and the rear wheels on one known vehicle have a diameter of 72 inches. The rear wheels of the Moose wagon measure 70 inches in diameter. (FIG. 26), and the rear wheels of the Hagley Museum wagon measure 68.5 inches. Wheels of this size usually have a tire width of 3.75 to 4 inches. Wagons of medium size typically have rear wheel diameters between 54 and 60 inches, and tire widths of 3 inches or more. Three large wagons that appear to be on original running gear, or at least on appropriate running gear, have front wheels of 48 inches diameter, and the Hagley Museum wagon has front wheels measuring 50 inches.

Sixteen spokes typically are found in the larger wheels, and fourteen in the wheels of medium size. Front wheels generally have but twelve spokes. It is said that three sets of wheels, large, medium, and small sometimes were made for the Conestogas that did double duty as farm and freight wagons, the medium and large wheels being used when the wagon was out on the road, and the small and medium wheels being used around the farm. The writers are not aware of any surviving wagon with its set of six original wheels.

The fellies of Conestoga wheels were short sections of oak sawn to shape, each piece containing but two spokes. In contrast, wheels of the late nineteenth century often had two semicircular fellies of steamed, bent oak. Wheel hubs, or naves, were turned from large single pieces of wood, often poplar. The spokes were carefully mortised into the hubs, and four iron bands were placed around the outside of the hub to bind it together. The conical hole in the center of the hub had a bushing of iron at either end to take the wear. These bushings, which properly are called boxes, are simply collars of iron with an iron fin on either side to prevent them from turning when mounted in the hub. In an advertisement in the Pittsburgh Gazette for 9 February, 1810 Rees E. Fleeson announced a general line of iron parts and castings for sale, including pots, kettles, irons, and "waggon boxes." Iron hub caps sometimes were used at the outer end of the wheel hub to keep dirt and dust away from the bearing surfaces.

The making of good wheels required the specialized talents of the wheelwright. Wheels usually were made with a small amount of "dish", i.e. the spokes did not lie in the plane of the tire but to one side of it. This complicated the making of the wheel but produced a stronger product. Wheel making called for a number of special tools and for considerable experience on the part of the maker. The subject cannot be pursued here, but it is considered in detail in a book entitled *The Wheelwright's Shop,* by G. Sturt.[2]

The "dish" proposely was put in a wagon wheel to give it a rigidity and an ability to resist lateral thrust that it would not have if the spokes all fell in the plane of the tire. The apex of the very shallow cone formed by the spokes is to the inside of the wheel as it is mounted on the wagon. On a poor road, where a wagon is made to lean to one side because one side of the road is higher than the other, a large lateral thrust on the wheel can be developed. This is resisted by the cone-shaped down-hill wheel, whose spokes are forced outward against the heavy iron tire. The plane of the tire for a mounted wheel is not vertical, but slightly inclined, away from the wagon box. When a wagon is viewed from behind, the rear wheels appear to lean away from the wagon. This is the necessary result of the dished wheel and the conical axle. In order that the wheel run true on the conical axle the lowest element of the axle cone is horizontal. This requires that the axis of the wheel be inclined downward, away from the wagon. It also allows the lowest spoke to be vertical and thus better able to carry the load directly above it, which is a most important consideration.

The traditional color used for the running gears and wheels was red, but as with the color of the wagon beds, there was no particular shade and hue that can be considered as the one and only authentic color. Oxide-red barn paint commonly is found on old running gears. Orange-colored red lead paint sometimes is found on them, but this is more typical of late-nineteenth century wagons. Sometimes a bright Chinese red color is found on them.

REFERENCES —

1. Searight, Thomas B. (1894) *The Old Pike, A History of the National Road:* T. B. Searight, Pub., Uniontown, Pa.
2. Sturt, G. (1923) *The Wheelwright's Shop:* Cambridge.

Chapter 16
Wagon Accessories

W HEN out on the long road, the wagoner had to be able to take care of the basic needs of his team and to maintain his wagon, so certain accessories became standard equipment on a Conestoga wagon. A water bucket was needed to provide for the horses; a jack and a tar pot full of tar were needed to keep the wheels rolling; the axe, which already has been discussed, was used for a number of purposes. A simple wooden bucket bound with iron was carried with the wagon so that the horses could be watered from any nearby water source. Watering troughs and rivers often were not convenient to the wagoner's overnight stopping place. Sometimes the bail of the bucket was hung on the rear extension of the coupling pole, which kept it well out of the way but handy when needed.

The feedbox, or feed trough, built of pine or poplar, is between five and six feet long, about twelve inches wide, and ten inches deep. The top edges of it are covered with light strap iron to keep it from being damaged by horses' teeth. At one end there is an iron lug which fits into a staple on the wagon tongue. At the other end is the pin which is placed in the doubletree pin hole on the tongue, to hold it firmly in place when used for feeding the horses. At the rear of the wagon bed there are two chains with hooks at the ends which fasten into rings at either end of the feedbox to hold it in traveling position against the lower part of the rear end gate.

Each wagon carried with it a wooden tar pot of characteristic shape (FIG. 68), which was used periodically to lubricate the axles of the wagon. These pots generally were turned from poplar logs. Each was provided with a lid of wood with a hole in the center through which stuck the handle of a wooden paddle used to apply the tar. The lubricant was a sticky mixture of pine tar and lard, which served the purpose and was easily acquired. It was applied directly to the axle, which required the removal of the wheel, hence the wagon jack found frequent use also. The tar pot was hung from a hook on the rear bolster by means of a leather thong, or sometimes by a chain, and sometimes a wide staple was placed on the axletree below the hook, to keep the pot from swaying excessively. The Pennsylvania Dutchman sometimes referred to his tar pot as a "schmutz pot" or as a "teer loedel."

Conestoga wagon jacks deserve particular attention because almost all of them bear the date of manufacture and a small amount of ornamentation, because some contain the maker's name or initials, and because they exhibit some variation of structure and shape as a function of time. They are rugged, almost indestructible, devices which have outlasted the wagons for which they were made. Their convenient size and the presence of dates on them makes them desirable antiques for collectors, and good mementos of the Conestoga century in lieu of a full size wagon.

The Conestoga jack presumably had its origins in central Europe, where jacks of similar structure probably were made in the late seventeenth and earliest part of the eighteenth centuries. The jack mechanism is almost identical to the mechanism of the crossbow cranequin in use in central Europe throughout the seventeenth century and in the sixteenth century as well (FIG. 69). In both devices the handle is attached to the shaft of a small four-toothed gear or pinion. This pinion meshes with a relatively large gear containing 18 teeth in the one wagon jack studied, and 43 teeth in the crossbow cranequin illustrated here. A small three-toothed gear is fastened on the same shaft as the large gear, and this meshes with the teeth of the rack.

The gears of the jack are confined within the iron plates that form the sides of the gear box, and the structure is riveted together, with permanence in mind. The body of the jack is wooden, and usually is of oak.

The mechanical advantage of a jack depends not only on the gearing, but also on the length of the crank that operates it. It is determined easily by counting the number of turns needed to move the rack a measured distance, and then determining the distance moved by the crank handle, which is the number of turns multiplied by the circumference of the crank circle. By dividing the distance the rack moves by the total distance covered by the crank, the mechanical advantage is found. This calculation was made for seven dated jacks, with the following results (dates are given in parentheses): (1794) 62.8; (1813) 76.3; (1821) 55; (1831) 59.4; (1836) 53.5; (1858) 78.5; (1889) 47. Typical values thus seem to lie between 50 and 80.

The total load on the rear wheel of a large Conestoga wagon laden with three and a half tons of goods would amount to about 2000 pounds. A jack with a mechanical advantage of 50 would require a force of merely 40 pounds to balance the wagon weight, assuming no friction, and for a mechanical advantage of 75 the balancing force is only 27 pounds.

Most jacks are equipped with a ratchet and pawl on the outside of the gear box, to hold the rack in the desired position when the jack is in use. Some early jacks lack this feature, however, and instead are equipped with a simple hook to hold the crank handle in position (see 1760 jack, FIG. 70). Other early jacks are equipped with the standard ratchet and pawl, but it is possible that some of these were added at a later date.

Dates on jacks of the Conestoga type range over a long span of years, from the early eighteenth century to almost the end of the eighteenth century (FIG. 70, 71). A jack on display at the Pennsylvania Farm Museum of Landis Valley bears the date of 1735, and Vincent Nolt of Lancaster declares that he once saw one dated 1729. One of the writers owns a jack dated 1889. The time between these two extreme dates is 160 years.

With the development of larger and heavier wagons in the period after about 1815, jacks became larger also. The body of the jack in the early period was relatively long and thin. A typical jack of the early period, bearing the date of 1794 (FIG. 70) has a body 20.5 inches high, 6.25 inches wide, and 3.5 inches thick. A large jack of the later period, dated 1836, has a height of 20 inches, a width of 9.5 inches, and a thickness of 3.75 inches. Mr. Don Berkebile of The Smithsonian Institution suggested to one of the writers that the period when the first large wagons came into existence might be inferred by noting the change in jack size as a function of time. To follow up this idea, the body dimensions of as many jacks as readily could be found, thirty in number, were determined. The most obvious variation in dimensions was in the relation of height to width, so the height-width ratio was studied as a function of the date of manufacture (FIG. 72). This revealed a distinct change in the height-width ratio after 1810. No data were available for the interval 1805-1810, but before 1805 all jacks had a height-width ratio of 3 or more, whereas all jacks made after 1810 had a height-width ratio of less than 3. This exact division probably is fortuitous, as a result of favorable and limited data, but nevertheless the trend suggested by the data is real. Throughout the eighteenth century a jack of remarkably standard proportions was made. In the decade between 1805 and 1815 relatively wider (and heavier) jacks made their appearance, and their manufacture continued throughout most of the remainder of the century. The same general trends are shown by data for the width of the jack body alone, and for the volume of the jack body. Inasmuch as the larger and heavier jacks probably were needed for the larger and heavier wagons, these data suggest that large Conestogas first made their appearance at about the time of the War of 1812. The classic period of Conestoga freighting over the mountains to the Ohio Valley began at about this time, and the National Road to Wheeling was completed in 1818. Apparently the large freighters appeared in response to the demands of economics after or during the time that good roads were made over the mountains.

Dates on wagon jacks are found on the vertical bar, or rack (FIG. 71). Although the jacks were made over a considerable range of time and by many different makers in many different places, the style of the date numerals, and the simple decorative patterns associated with the dates, follow a standard traditional pattern. A pointed punch, a straight chisel, and one or two curved chisels were used to form the numerals and designs. Above the date numerals a cross-hatched pattern usually is present, with the intersections of the lines accentuated by punch marks. A single punch mark often is found at the center of each quadrangle or triangle between these lines. Below the date initials or even the name of the maker sometimes are found. At the bottom, below the date, and initials, a pyramid of punch marks usually is found.

The numeral one of the date sometimes is made as a simple vertical line, but usually it has a special form that is characteristic of jacks and which is not found on other dated objects of early America. This special jack numeral is in the form of a double I crossed, or a double J crossed, with the second J reversed (FIG. 71). H. K. Landis[3] suggested that this special figure meant "Jahr Herr Jesu", and this may well be the explanation for it, however it seems likely that the figure would have been widely used on a variety of other dated objects made in the land of the Pennsylvania Dutch if this explanation is valid. Possibly the use of this special numeral was simply a tradition that got started among blacksmiths in the early eighteenth century and

FIGURE 71. Dated wagon jacks span more than a century and a half of time. The dates shown here are 1736, 1749, 1756, 1760, 1794, 1809, 1813, 1831, 1836, and 1858. A jack of 1735 is on display at the Pennsylvania Farm Museum of Landis Valley, and one dated 1889 is owned by G. Shumway. *Penna. Farm Museum of Landis Valley; Shelburne Museum, Inc.; W. S. Redhed.*

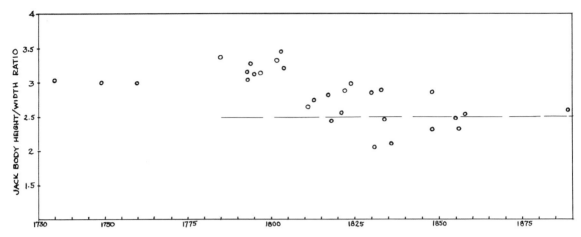

FIGURE 72. Early jacks are relatively narrow in comparison with later jacks. This is reflected in the ratio of height to width. The relatively wide and heavy jacks were made for the heavy wagons used between 1815 and 1850.

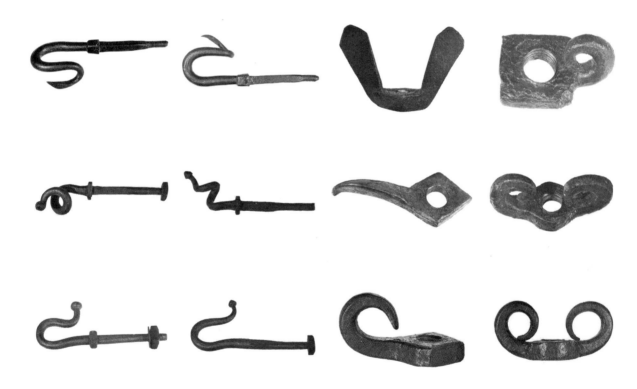

FIGURE 73. Blacksmith artistry is shown by elaborate stay chain hooks and wing nuts from Conestoga wagons.

was carried on by others in later years. It is found on the latest known jack, of date 1889. A variation of the standard figure has the cross bar connected to the reversed J, forming one continuous curve (see 1760 jack, FIG. 71).

The wagon jack traveled with the wagon on its long trips, but neither the bed nor the running gear contained any special rack or place to hold the jack. The toolbox usually was too small to hold the jack, so the only possible place for the jack to be kept was inside the wagon bed, among the goods that were being hauled. The jack had to be accessible to the wagoner, so it probably was kept near the rear end gate where it could be reached by removing the gate.

In addition to the standard accessories, a number of tools and repair parts probably were carried along, and the place for them to be kept was the toolbox. There is no record from days of old to tell us what a toolbox contained, but it is likely that the items listed below often were found there (FIG. 66). Horseshoes, nails, a horseshoe hammer, a clinching iron, and a hoof rasp might well have been carried to keep the team in traveling condition. Snaps, cockeyes, and a spare bit would have been useful harness accessories. Other possible toolbox items include pincers, an extra linch pin or two, assorted washers, nuts, bolts, and nails, some staples, a corncob to use in the wheel hub to keep a loose linch pin from jumping out, eelskin for harness repairs, middle rings, and open links. A Little Brown Jug and a gimlet would have been used, perhaps, by a wagoner to steal his whiskey supply from the whiskey barrels he hauled. To do this he would force up a hoop, bore a hole with his gimlet, fill the jug, plug the hole, and replace the hoop. Perhaps a horse chestnut also was carried along, to ward off rheumatism.

REFERENCE —

1. Omwake, John (1930) *The Conestoga Six-horse Bell Teams of Eastern Pennsylvania:* John Omwake, Publisher, Cincinnati.

ACKNOWLEDGMENTS

In addition to those persons acknowledged in the Foreword, there are a number of others who have helped in one way or another with the production of this book. Many persons, organizations, and institutions contributed photographs of wagons and accessories, and we wish to thank them collectively. We have indicated with the captions to the figures the sources of most of the photographs and drawings. Mr. Nick Eggenhofer, well-known artist of the American western scene, and author of his own book on wagons, *Wagons, Mules, and Men* (Hastings House, Publishers, 1961), made the drawing used for the end plates and also the drawings for FIGURES 44, 45, 46, 47, 60, 61. Mr. Albert I. Drachman contributed Chapter 10 and in addition, gave permission to quote at length from his paper published in 1955. Mr. Don H. Berkebile of the Transportation Division, Smithsonian Institution was especially helpful in discussing the subject matter of the book with the senior author and in reviewing a preliminary version of the manuscript.

INDEX